enjoy
life outside

INSPIRED
PROJECTS

by Linda Bodo

**15 DIY
AL FRESCO
ENCOUNTERS**

enjoy
life outside

INSPIRED
PROJECTS

by Linda Bodo

**15 DIY
AL FRESCO
ENCOUNTERS**

e

Printed in Canada 5   4   3   2   1

Library and Archives Canada Cataloguing in Publication

Bodo, Linda, 1957–
Enjoy life outside, inspired projects : DIY al fresco encounters/Linda Bodo.
Includes index.

ISBN 978-1-894728-08-9

1. Gardens—Design. I. Title.
SB473.B63 2008   712'.6   C2008-907291-X

Published by Enjoy Books
101 Bellerose Drive
St. Albert, Alberta, Canada T8N 8N8
www.enjoygardening.com

Enjoy Books is an imprint of Hole's Publishing

Publication Management: Bruce Timothy Keith
Editor: Christina McDonald
Editorial Development: Jean Coulton and Leslie Vermeer
Book and cover design: Carol Dragich, Dragich Design
Photography: Akemi Matsubuchi

DISCLAIMER

Due to differing conditions, materials, tools, and individual skills, Hole's Greenhouses & Gardens Ltd. assumes no responsibility for any damages, injuries suffered, or losses incurred as a result of attempting any suggested projects. Always read and observe safety precautions provided by manufacturers, and follow all accepted safety procedures.

FOR DAD

Your passion inspired me to follow in your extraordinary footsteps. Through your never-ending support, patience, and tutelage, this book has become reality.

Contents

THE PROJECTS

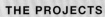

DISCOVERY

It was December 31, 1963, and my parents and I had braved one of Montreal's classic winter blizzards in Dad's '59 Dodge panel van to attend the New Year's Eve festivities in the basement of the Hungarian United Church.

We almost didn't make it. Waist high drifts and impassable roads threatened, but, thankfully, I arrived in plenty of time to sip ginger ale from champagne glasses and don the celebratory headgear. I giggled when Dad asked me to dance, then took his hand as he led me to the parquet floor. I looked up nervously for direction. Without missing a beat, my father scooped me up in his arms and lowered me onto his well-polished oxfords where I learned the principles of the two-step. In no time at all, I was leading. I discovered confidence.

I was in Grade 4 when I got my first bike. It was a splendid specimen—a low rider with a yellow banana seat, long handlebars, and shiny chrome fenders. For the better part of a week each night after dinner, Dad would haul my bike down the three storeys of our walk-up apartment for a few hours of driver training in our small suburban neighbourhood. With his patient support, I finally managed to solo down the gravel-lined alley, my heart pounding in my chest. I felt the exhilaration build as I peddled faster and faster, leaving Dad grinning behind me in a cloud of dust. I discovered courage.

There was an almost surreal order to Dad's immaculate workshop, brightly lit with salvaged electrical components rescued from trash cans and demolitions. Orderly shelves filled with orphaned plumbing parts and labelled cans—brimming with fasteners, washers, and thingamabobs—lined the walls. Tools were fastidiously parked in their allotted stalls, facilitated by silhouettes he had traced around each and every implement. The smell of varnish filled the air as finishing touches were applied to masterpieces coaxed from forgotten planks of wood. The power tools, screaming creatures of metal with steel fangs that spit billows of fine dust, both fascinated and terrified me. But as I watched things come to life in my father's practiced hands, I hungered to possess his magical touch. Under his guidance, I began to take matters into my own hands. I discovered creativity.

DIY: a medley of glue, gadgets, and guts tossed with equal amounts of confidence, courage, and creativity.

DIWise

A completed project should not be measured by the time it took to accomplish, but by the sheer delight of achieving it.

Remember that the next time you glue your finger to a two-by-four.

Years later, the prop design field beckoned. Here was an opportunity to partner my passion for DIY with the art of visual presentation. With a degree under my tool belt, I developed a successful freelance business that morphed into a full-service prop design and manufacturing company. For the next three decades, as founder of PROPabilities Corp, I had the time of my life "imagineering" dreams into reality for shopping malls, convention centres, and trade shows. Pioneering the field of prop production in Edmonton, Alberta, gave me a grand opportunity to create faux replicas while honing skills bestowed by my father. The journey made me uniquely suited to adapting unusual materials into DIY projects at home, and I began to cultivate my signature style. In time, I retraced my steps back to the home workshop, to shift gears from large corporate projects to more manageable undertakings that anyone could produce. Whether writing a monthly lifestyle column, contributing DIY articles to magazines, or addressing enthusiastic audiences, I aspire to inspire "The Art of Living."

I absorbed my father's wisdom for 40-odd years. We created a veritable hive of activity—a swarm of two that moved mantles, mandrills, and mountains. We met at least once a week, sharing countless hours at the hardware store, downing gallons of espresso while checking measurements, and repeatedly cursing Murphy's Law whenever it reared its ugly head.

As I put the finishing touches on this book, I glance about my own workshop. Dad would have approved. Paraphernalia dangles from the ceiling over fastidiously labelled and organized cupboards, coffee cans sort bits and bobs, and a pretty impressive inventory of power tools lines the shelves. It's here that sorry specimens destined for the dump are rescued and repurposed. In this DIY test kitchen, I continue my father's legacy of pairing unique materials to repurpose them into operational works of art.

Through a gruelling process of product testing, fine tuning, and occasional head scratching, I have compiled some of my favourite projects for your outdoor living spaces. You do not have to be a finishing carpenter, licensed electrician, or professional painter to complete any of these undertakings. The "guess" has been taken out of the "work" to generate projects that anyone can achieve while using everyday objects that are easily sourced. Simple steps are combined with crisp photography and straightforward illustrations to be easy to follow. The only challenge on your part is deciding which project to start. Let my sweat build your equity. Discover your confidence, courage, and creativity.

Linda Bodo

DO IT YOURSELF

Why DIY? Stress relief, an outlet for creativity, a sense of accomplishment...the list is endless. The emphasis on the home and all things domestic has made us hungry for items touched by human hands, handcrafted with charming imperfections, rare in value. It is time to repurpose, recycle, and redefine your leisure time.

Consider DIY a form of occupational therapy and switch off from the daily grind through the whack of a hammer or the rev of a power tool. Trade in your computer or BlackBerry for a glue gun or a Dremel tool, and transform raw materials into unique accoutrements for the home and garden. Follow a project through from start to finish—it can be infinitely more rewarding than clearing that stack of paperwork from your desk. Roll up your sleeves and get dirty. Find your passion. Become a DIY enthusiast.

JUST DO IT

The DIY concept has been around as long as we have. DIY was a necessary skill for self-sufficiency and a means to barter for goods, services, and dowries. Simple tools and local resources provided the raw materials essential for creating a shelter and making a life.

The dawn of the Industrial Revolution triggered a huge shift in DIY culture. Assembly-line wares became the order of the day as homeowners opted to purchase store-bought facsimiles to articulate their personal style. Fast-forward to the 1960s when nationwide branding through commercials had us glued to TV screens, drooling over polyester leisure suits and mini-length wedding dresses. Unique and handmade was out; conformist and mass produced was in. By the late 1980s, our attentions were further diverted from DIY with the advent of the Internet and specialty television channels that had us honing our skills at typing and dialling 1–800 numbers. The time has come to renew our vows with DIY and put a personal stamp on our home's footprint. Mark your territory.

The DIY culture is not all about learning; it's also about doing. Few of us have a job where we can produce a tangible commodity at the end of the day. When you build something, you experience a sense of pride and achievement, something to show for your effort, something concrete. Contrary to popular belief, DIY is not just about saving money; it's about satisfaction and creation. One cannot put a price on this.

The projects in this book are intended to inspire. Once you have conquered the easier ones, consider taking on something more ambitious. Tailor selected projects to best suit your tastes by altering sizes, materials, or finishes. Encourage family or friends to join in the fun, and motivate them with your new-found skills. Concrete isn't just for driveways and two-by-fours can do far more than frame a room.

DO IT OUT OF DOORS

The welcome seasonal pause from the rigours of cold weather brings with it that most treasured commodity in the northern hemisphere: outdoor living. Say goodbye to woollies and hello to longer days, sunshine, and a break from work or school.

Neighbours drop by and an afternoon is spent playing *boules* while sipping on mint-infused mojitos. The scent of freshly mown grass is thick in the air as friends gather for an impromptu dinner amid the chorus of crickets. A circle of chairs is hastily arranged around a firepit where s'mores are wrapped in foil, then carefully toasted. Time comes and goes; your pulse slows and your mind clears. You are in the zone, reconnecting with family, friends, and your soul.

Blurring the boundaries between inside and out is not exclusive to homeowners. It's for anyone who hankers for personalized and comfortable surroundings. A *plein air* sanctuary can be as simple as a balcony, as decadent as a rooftop terrace, or as casual as a porch or veranda. Parlay a patio with chic lighting, bedeck a deck with comfy seating, or garnish a garden with custom-made stepping stones.

Use your space as a means of communication between yourself and Mother Nature, a pause between interior confinement and exterior freedom. Outdoors, the sky is the limit.

It has been said that it is better to give than receive, so why not give something handmade from the heart? Several of the garden accessories in this book are perfect for gift giving and sure to impress. Consider donating a garden embellishment as an auction item for your favourite charity, or create a series of table centrepieces for a dear one's wedding or anniversary celebration. Make it personal.

Although the walk down the aisle from raw materials to completed project is self-rewarding, revelling at your accomplishments is infinitely better. Stage your masterpiece, engage in a little back patting, and pose for photos. This is the best part of the ceremony.

DON'T DO IT WITHOUT

No self-respecting DIY aficionado can function properly without the appropriate tools. Invest in a few essentials and expand your kit as needed. Always use the correct tools for the job; using a screwdriver as a chisel could result in blood, sweat, and tears. On the following page, I've included a list for a basic tool kit, a few handy helpers to round out your collection, and a special wish list you may want to ask Santa to fill this Christmas.

Power tools are "the great levellers" between the sexes. Today, many power tools are cheaper than take-out and can improve the ease and speed of a job considerably. You may never have been exposed to them, but with the help of a little safety training there is nothing to fear.

Aprons and tool belts, although not strictly necessary, do keep gear close at hand and save rummaging through layers of assembled material for a pencil or tape measure. As far as caring for tools goes, remember to keep bits, blades, and cutters sharp and stored properly so that you won't nick yourself. I stress this point because dull tools require extra force and can bind, making them dangerous and a pain to operate.

HANDY & HELPFUL

Jigsaw and circular saw

Specialized drill bits (e.g., Forstner) and paddle attachment

Caulking gun

Glue gun and glue sticks

Clamps

Wood and metal files

Tile cutter, nippers, notched trowel, and spatulas

Large utility pails

Paint brushes, rollers, trays, and rags

DIYer's WISH LIST

Band saw

Chop saw or cut-off saw

Portable table saw

Drill press

Belt sander

Dremel tool

7" wet saw

Shop vacuum

Angle grinder

THE MUST HAVES

Hammer and assorted nails

Electric drill and assorted drill bits

Screwdrivers and assorted screws

Pliers

Scissors, utility knife, and blades

Wire cutters

Straight edge, square, and level

Tape measure

Pencil or chalk

Handsaw and hacksaw

Stapler and staples

Sanding block and sandpapers

Toolbox

Gloves, mask, safety goggles, and ear protection

I want to remind you that if you're lacking a skill or a tool, staff at the hardware store can be quite accommodating. Just ask them to cut lumber or pipe for you. If you are going to use a specialty tool once, borrow it from a friend or neighbour, or rent it for an afternoon instead of forking out the dough to buy it. And if you're not into foraging in the woods for twigs, branches, or other organic supplies, don't forget about your local garden centre or craft outlet.

THE WORKSHOP

A workshop can be as elaborate as a stand-alone studio or as simple as a corner in a spare bedroom. Good light, ventilation, and a bit of space to spread out and move about are essential. If you have young children or inquisitive pets, a room with a locking door is a must.

Working on a raised surface will save serious wear and tear on your back. Customize the height of your work surface by raising it up on blocks, and expand accessibility by adding locking casters. You can fabricate a basic workbench from sawhorses and a sheet of plywood so it can be taken down for storage when not needed. Using a swing-arm desk lamp can enhance overhead lighting. If you are working outside, picnic tables or potting benches can play double duty as sturdy worktops.

My workshop is an organized, defined space where I spend a lot of time. I purchased and installed rubber floor tiles from the hardware store, and they're warm and comfortable to stand on. When I'm not standing, I have a tall stool to perch on, and I keep a folding stepladder nearby to retrieve safely items stored high up in the old kitchen cabinets I've mounted on the walls. I keep a stack of drop sheets to protect surfaces in case I need to spread a project out on the floor. I use a large bin for garbage but, in order to save my back, I never overfill it. Another bin neatly contains scraps of lumber. I'm big on safety (see Safety Do's and Don'ts, page 10) and keep all of my safety equipment close at hand. I also have music playing, which adds to an enjoyable atmosphere.

DIWise
There are no mistakes in the DIY workshop, only experiments.

SAFETY DO'S AND DON'TS

Take the time to review the following safety tips to avoid trips to the emergency department. As a bonus, you'll look like a pro with all the gear.

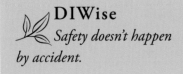
DIWise
Safety doesn't happen by accident.

1. **Wear safety goggles, work gloves, and a dust mask** when working with power tools, sanders, saws, paint, or concrete. Always wear hearing protection when operating loud or repetitive equipment.

2. **Equip your workshop with a fire extinguisher** and periodically check the charge. Keep a well-stocked first aid kit on hand. A basic first aid poster is great in an emergency, as is a shop phone.

3. **If possible, work outdoors** when painting, sanding, or cutting materials. If it is too cold, work indoors in a well-ventilated space.

4. **Always cut away from yourself** when using cutting tools.

5. **Unplug power tools** when changing blades or bits, or when cleaning. Don't use electrical tools outside when it's raining. Check that all electrical cords are in good shape. It may be well worth the effort to have damaged cords replaced on good power tools, but don't put this task off.

6. **Ladders are one of the main causes of DIY accidents.** Position ladders on flat, firm surfaces, and keep your weight centred. Never stand on the top two rungs.

7. **Dispose of rubbish carefully.** Before disposing of rags soaked with paint thinner or other flammable liquids, lay them out flat to dry, just as you would a favourite sweater. Carelessness may lead to fire due to spontaneous combustion.

8. **Don't wear loose clothing or open-toed shoes.** Fabric can catch on machinery, and a dropped tool or piece of lumber can really hurt your feet.

9. **Read all instructions and warning labels** on tools and materials before using for the first time. Keep operating manuals organized in an easy-to-access place.

10. **Keep the workshop floor clear and clean** to avoid tripping or slipping. Coil and hang electrical cords, sweep up messes promptly, and store brooms upright or mounted on the wall.

DOING IT RIGHT

Here are a few tips, tidbits, and tactics intended to save time and make any job more pleasurable. It's always easier to learn from the trials and tribulations of others.

1. **Find a partner to split material costs.** Some projects require just a few metres of lumber or small amounts of cement, but you may only be able to purchase these supplies in standard lengths or quantities.

2. **Get your head around a project before you start.** Read through the instructions from start to finish. This will save time, eliminate nasty surprises, and reduce frustration levels.

3. **The French call it *mise en place*, or everything in place**. In relation to cooking it refers to gathering, measuring, and cutting all of the ingredients required for a recipe before you begin cooking. Applied to DIY, it means setting out all the tools and materials needed before commencing a project.

4. **Lay out all your patterns before cutting** to be sure to make the most of your materials with as little waste as possible.

5. **Only a fool rushes in.** Pay attention to drying and curing schedules and follow recommended time frames. Failure to do so could result in peeling, bubbling, or shrinkage.

6. **Remember to recycle, repurpose, and reuse.** Baskets and battens, sticks and stones, vents and vessels can all be transformed into something marvellous.

7. **Pace yourself.** If the loud gurgle echoing from your tummy reminds you that dinner was two hours ago, stop and pack up for the day. Remember, you are trying to have fun. Save your enthusiasm for the next session and go have a bite to eat.

8. **These projects do not have to outlive your great grandchildren,** be impervious to the elements, or be Superman strong. Their role is to enhance your lifestyle through personal creativity. Remember, you can always whip up a replacement.

SOURCES
Track down materials, textiles, embellishments, and antiquities at the following sources:

- Antique shops and flea markets
- Architectural clearing houses
- Auctions and bazaars
- Big-box chains and hardware outlets
- Consignment shops and pawnshops
- Craft and hobby retailers
- Dollar stores
- Estate and garage sales
- Fabric shops
- Habitat for Humanity ReStores
- Upholstery suppliers

DIWise
Critical path thinking saves time, tempers, and thumbs.

TIMBERRRRR

WORKING WITH WOOD

You don't have to be a master carpenter to coax a creation from wood. This organic and forgiving medium lends itself to a variety of functions, which can be achieved with the simplest of tools.

1. **Consider safety and your well-being at all times.** Protect your hearing when working with loud or repetitive machinery. Don safety goggles when cutting, drilling, or sanding wood. Look for impact-resistant lenses, preferably those with side screens for the ultimate protection. Use a mask or respirator when sanding or cutting wood, particularly when working with pressure-treated wood. Avoid injury when working with power tools by wearing long, tailored sleeves, pants, and proper footwear.

2. **Take time at the lumber store** to choose straight, knot-free pieces of wood. Whenever possible, store lumber horizontally to prevent warping. Sand off markers and stamps before you begin cutting.

3. **To drive screws easily into wood and prevent splitting, pre-drill pilot holes** half the diameter of the screw size in hard woods, and one-quarter the diameter in soft woods.

4. **When drilling holes in wood, back the piece with scrap wood to minimize splintering when the bit breaks through.** Clear chips from the hole as you drill to keep the bit working at maximum capacity and allow clear visibility.

5. **Measure twice, cut once, really.** Cut your wood with the "best face" down when using a circular or chop saw, and cut with the "best face" up when using a table saw. Apply masking tape over cutting lines to prevent splintering.

6. **To cut a large opening in a sheet of wood, begin by tracing your pattern onto the wood.** Drill a pilot hole in the centre of your pattern with a drill bit large enough to accommodate a jigsaw blade. Put the blade in the pilot hole and follow the traced pattern.

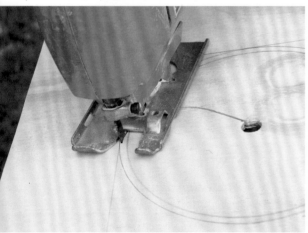

7. **Always sand with the grain of wood using even strokes and pressure.** Remove dust with a tack cloth or damp rag. Do not be tempted to purchase the least expensive sandpaper available. You will end up using more sheets for the task and a great deal of time changing the paper on your sander. Buy aluminium oxide paper; in the long run it will save money, time, and your nerves.

8. **For smooth, even surfaces, fill gaps and open-grained woods with exterior wood filler.** Use a small spatula to apply wood filler and work it into crevices. Once the wood filler loses its sheen and begins to harden, remove any excess with a damp cloth. Sand surfaces smooth. If necessary, repeat the process until the desired effect is achieved.

9. **Be sure to use exterior-grade wood glues for wood-based projects that will be used outdoors.** Also choose galvanized hardware, nails, and screws that won't rust.

10. **Wood can be finished with a variety of products: stain, paint, polyurethane varnish, or oil.** Keep wood scraps to use as testers for finishes. If you're custom blending your paint or stain, be sure to write down your recipes.

CONCRETE EVIDENCE

WORKING WITH CEMENT

Cement is a wonderful material for creating all kinds of durable projects, but it seems to intimidate many DIYers. Once you've had a little practice working with different types of cement, you'll be sure to think of all sorts of different uses for it.

1. **Safety first.** Dry cement is caustic and when mixed with water to become the product we know as concrete, it becomes even more so. Be sure to wear long sleeves and pants, waterproof gloves, eye protection, and a respiratory mask when handling all types of cement. Work outdoors when possible, or in a well-ventilated area if inside. Employ the same safety procedures when staining concrete with acid.

2. **Pre-measure dry ingredients.** Mix and store ingredients in pails to save time when preparing wet solution.

3. **For extra torque when mixing concrete recipes, use an electric drill** with a paddle attachment instead of a cordless model.

4. **The percentage of water added to a concrete mix is the main factor affecting the strength and quality of the finished piece.** Less water produces stronger concrete. However, a stiff mix does not easily settle into the nooks and crannies of detailed undertakings. Aim for a balance between a thick and thin, muffin-batter texture. Ridges should form when a stick or paddle is run through the mixture. If the mixture is too wet and ridges don't appear, add a little more dry mix.

5. **Keep a pail of water nearby when mixing concrete to soak the paddle between uses.** Clean up spills promptly and protect floor surfaces with a drop cloth.

6. **Concrete mixes harden at different rates, depending on temperature and percentage of cement in the mix.** The more cement, the faster the cure. The warmer the air temperature, and/or the warmer the water added to the dry mix, the quicker the set time. Aim for a slow, cool, and damp cure to produce strong, durable products.

7. **Always work on a level surface when pouring concrete.**

8. **Pour leftover concrete mix into plastic cups** or inverted paper party hats to create samples for fine-tuning acid stains or sealant finishes.

9. **Concrete can be coloured in different ways:** by acid staining, which is applied to a finished project, or by the use of additives, which are added to the dry components before mixing with water. Acid staining concrete will produce a natural, mottled finish. Apply acid stain with a spray bottle according to manufacturer's instructions. Mix several colours together to create a marbleized effect. Dry 24 hours. Rinse and scrub off acid residue in a water bath with mild detergent. Repeat stain/wash process until desired effect is achieved. The more stain you apply, the darker the finish. After the final rinse, dry 24 hours and seal with two coats of sealant. A concrete supply store can provide a variety of iron oxide pigments as additives to achieve a uniform colour throughout your concrete. Simply add to the basic recipe when mixing.

10. **Sealing concrete helps to protect the finish but it is not always necessary.**

THE TILE FILE

WORKING WITH TILE

Installing ceramic tile is easy with fast-setting thinset or mastic adhesives, grout, and sealants. Whatever style or size of tile you choose to install, the principles are the same. Tools and materials include work gloves, rubber gloves, adhesive, grout sealer, tiles, a grooved trowel, a grout float, tile nippers, a tile cutter, a rubber squeegee, a sponge, and a level. Inspiration for designs can come from a wide range of sources, from a favourite dinner plate to a grand museum mosaic.

1. **Safety is always the first consideration.** Wear goggles and well-fitted work gloves when cutting tile. Tile edges are sharp, and small shards can cause serious damage to your eyes.

2. **Be sure that the surface to be tiled is free of loose dirt, dust, peeling paint, and grease.** Scuff with sandpaper. Apply two coats of Red Gard waterproofing membrane to the base surface if project will be exposed to water.

3. **Conduct a dry run with your tiles by laying out your design and cutting all pieces before adhering.** You can do this directly on the piece to be tiled or you can use an identically sized scrap piece. The latter choice allows you to work smoothly without fear of disturbing the design. Mark two centre lines vertically and horizontally on your surface to act as a guide for your design.

4. **A manual tile cutter can easily handle most cutting jobs,** but if you are cutting a lot of tiles and have access to a wet saw, it can save time.

5. **Mix thinset or mastic adhesive according to manufacturer's instructions.** Spread as much adhesive as you'll be able to cover with tiles in a half hour. As you progress, spread more adhesive as needed. Apply with a notched trowel, holding the trowel at a 45-degree angle. The notches on the trowel help to ensure an even distribution of adhesive. Starting on the middle cross-line reference, transfer the tiles onto the adhesive, gently pressing down. Leave a ¼" gap between tiles or use plastic tile spacers for even distances. Periodically check your work to make sure that tiles are level.

6. **Clean up any excess thinset or mastic from work area with warm water.** Allow adhesives to dry 24 hours before grouting.

7. **Mix grout according to the manufacturer's instructions.** Spread a liberal amount of grout onto the tile and work it into the joints with a grout float. Hold the float at a 45-degree angle and spread the grout in several directions to ensure it settles into all the gaps.

8. **When grout sets up and forms a haze on the tile,** use a damp sponge to wipe away the excess from the tile surface.

9. **Allow the grout to cure based on the manufacturer's recommendations,** then apply two or three coats of grout sealant.

STICKY SITUATIONS

WORKING WITH ADHESIVES

Glue is a DIYer's best friend and the most common fastener. Using the proper adhesive for a project will ensure a successful result. Read the instructions on the label for the appropriate applications and use.

1. **Glues often have specific storage temperature ranges** that help them maintain their effectiveness. This means if your workshop reaches freezing temperatures, you should store glue elsewhere.

2. **Wait for excess wood glue to gel before removing from around joins.** Wiping before gelling will spread adhesive into wood and require extra sanding. Use small paintbrushes or wood scraps to spread glue. Always wipe the spouts of containers and replace lids securely after use.

3. **Multi-purpose spray adhesives work best when applied in light, thorough coatings.** Place the project on a drop sheet for easy cleanup of any overspray. Clean nozzles after use by tipping the can upside down and spraying until adhesive does not emit, then wiping the nozzle with a cloth. Work in a well-ventilated area.

4. **Keep heated glue guns upright to prevent damaging the thermostat.** Use hot glue with extreme caution—keep a bowl of cold water handy in case of a burn. Remove glue hairs with a hair dryer set on its hottest temperature.

5. **When using caulk, lay a thin bead of material using steady motion and applying constant pressure.** Smooth the bead and remove excess caulk with the tip of a spoon or the corner of a credit card. Tidy up any lap marks with a moist finger.

PAINTS AND TINTS

WORKING WITH COLOURANT

The finishing touches of any project are the most rewarding. Paints, stains, sealants, and waxes can add depth, the impression of years of wear, or a gentle patina. Always use exterior finishes for any projects intended for outdoors.

1. **Wear gloves, a respirator, and goggles** when painting, staining, or sealing. Use spray paints in a well-ventilated room or outdoors on a still day.

2. **Opt for paints that are water-based** or display a low VOC (volatile organic compound) content. VOCs are solvents that evaporate and contribute to the depletion of the ozone.

3. **Take empty paint cans to a recycling depot** that handles both the container and its contents. Never pour paint thinner or paint down the drain.

4. **Tightly fasten lids on paint cans and store upside down.** This treatment will form a seal around the lid to keep paint fresh and ease the process of mixing when you set the can upright for use. For an airtight closure, place a layer of plastic wrap over the opening before tapping the lid into place. Do not allow paint, stain, wax, or varnish to freeze.

5. **Avoid clogged spray paint nozzles** by turning the can upside down and spraying until the stream turns clear, then wiping the nozzle with a cloth.

6. **If you plan to paint a project over several days, wrap your brush, roller, or paint tray in plastic to keep surfaces moist.** For smaller projects, cover paint trays with plastic wrap before adding paint and, when finished, simply discard the wrap for a quick clean up.

7. **When you are painting, work logically.** Paint and stain with the grain. Always paint, stain, or seal the back or bottom of a project first to prevent scratching or marring on the front face. Elevate your work from the working surface to prevent sticking or drips from accumulating on edges. Styrofoam blocks are handy for supporting screws and hardware while you paint. Clamps or vices wrapped in plastic will hold unstable items steady while you work.

8. **Allow surfaces to dry thoroughly between coats.** If necessary, lightly sand and wipe between coats.

9. **Create your own custom colours** by adding universal professional tints to paints. These colourants are available wherever paints are sold and come in handy 4-oz. tubes. You can also add tints to wax to create darker shades for an aged finish.

10. **Seal a project with wax** to produce a subtle old-world sheen.

PENNY FOR YOUR THOUGHTS

WORKING WITH COPPER

Copper is soft metal that is easy to work with. It is available in a variety of forms: wire, foil, sheet, or tubing. Wear work gloves when handling sharp-edged sheets of copper.

1. **There are two types of copper tubing, hard and soft.** One kind of hard tubing is type M, the most common type of copper pipe sold. It is thin walled and marked with red lettering. Another kind is type L, which is thicker walled and is used for providing water services or where the pipe will be exposed. It is marked with blue lettering. Soft copper pipe is referred to as refrigeration tubing.

2. **Working with copper pipe requires standard tools.** A pipe cutter gives a straight, clean cut, but you can substitute with a hacksaw.

3. **To use a pipe cutter,** first hand-tighten it to the pipe and then rotate it around the pipe a couple of times to create a groove that encircles the pipe. Each time you rotate the cutter, tighten the blade a little. Each rotation will cut a little deeper into the pipe and the cut will be straight. Don't tighten too much or you may bend the pipe out of round.

4. **After cutting pipe, be sure to remove any burrs** with a round file, 60-grit sandpaper, or a Dremel fitted with a file attachment. This step will ensure proper adhesion of parts.

5. **If you find torches intimidating, use Just-for-Copper adhesive** to join copper segments. Follow the manufacturer's instructions for a waterproof connection.

6. **You can track down copper sheeting at metal supermarkets,** which are located in most major centres. These retailers purchase odds and ends from industry fabricators and resell to the public in small quantities. Orders are generally cut to size while you wait.

7. **Save copper wire scraps.** They can be twisted and coiled to create embellishments, hooks, and handles for your projects.

WRAPPING IT UP

WINTERIZING PROJECTS

Extend the life of your outdoor projects by storing them appropriately over the winter. Depending on your region, the amount of protection needed may vary. Move furniture projects into a shed or if very large, as in the case of the potting bench on page 60, secure a tarp around it with bungee cords.

Precautions should be taken to ensure that water does not freeze in fountains and cause them to crack or to damage pumps during the cold winter months. Prior to the first freeze of the season, drain your fountain completely. Remove the pump, clean it, and store it indoors in a bucket filled with water so that the seals and gaskets do not dry out. If possible, disassemble your fountain and place it in a shed or garage to protect it from damaging weather. If indoor storage is not practical, cover your fountain with a tarp or other protective material and fill the basin with material such as burlap or blankets to absorb any condensation that may accumulate and freeze during the winter.

ABOUT THE PROJECTS

MEASUREMENTS

Metric is the official standard of measurement in Canada, but lumber, pipe, hardware, and tools are still sold in imperial measures. For this reason, all of my projects are created using imperial measurements.

SKILL LEVEL

I've rated each project according to difficulty (simple, intermediate, and challenging). You can tell which is which by following the graphic legend to the right.

- simple
- intermediate
- challenging

TIMELINE AND VALUE

I've also provided a loose timeline for creating the projects and assigned a rough value comparing the DIY cost to an approximate retail price.

TIMELINE
1 hour

VALUE
DIY $10–30
Suggested retail $75

Raking It In
TOOL OBELISK

Spring arrives in a shower of sunshine that soaks the earth with the promise of longer days and that dreaded of all phenomena, spring cleaning. Shards of sunlight cascade through hazy windows, highlighting the results of winter's extended stay with alarming intensity. Clearly, a few days of hard work are in order. While fresh blades of grass tidy up brown lawns and unfurling buds dress otherwise naked trees, you chase dust bunnies, deconstruct cobwebs, and buff every conceivable surface to a five-star rating. Nothing has evaded your eagle eyes, no matter how cunningly disguised, and the victory encourages you to tackle matters outdoors.

Old tools that have been relegated to the far corners of your shed or garage can be repurposed as primitive elements in your landscape. Creating focal points with rustic components is a great way to recycle and put heart and soul back into your garden. Craft that classic garden accoutrement, the obelisk, with worn tools such as rakes, hoes, and pitchforks. These towers are perfect for edible climbers or ornamental vines. Leave the tripods in place over winter to add a sculptural element to an otherwise stark landscape. It is a surefire way to drive the winter blues away until next year's spring ritual.

TIMELINE
1 hour

VALUE
DIY $10–30
Suggested retail $75

MATERIALS
Three rusty garden
  implements
  (rakes, hoes, or forks)
Heavy wire or large tie
  wraps
Twine or raffia
Finishing wax or
  sealant stain

TOOLS
Wire cutters
Scissors

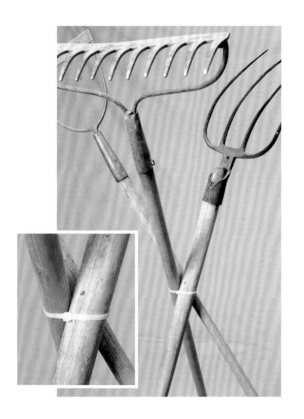

CLIMBING VINES

For those of us with fickle hearts, annual climbing vines are rewarding plants to grow. We can experiment each year with a new variety of bean or flower without guilt. I think this obelisk is particularly well suited to old-fashioned favourites like this black-eyed Susan vine (*Thunbergia elata*). It grows quickly from seed planted right after all danger of frost has passed or you can start it indoors to get a jump on spring. The 'Sunny' series grows five feet high, and two or three plants are more than sufficient to smother the obelisk.

STEP BY STEP

1. Wax or stain the handles of three garden implements to help preserve them from damp soil and the elements.

2. With the handles pointing down, create a tripod by tying the tools together with heavy wire or tie wraps at about one-quarter of the tools' length from the heads. Cover the strapping with twine or raffia for a decorative effect.

3. Position the obelisk in the garden with the legs pulled apart. Slightly bury the legs in the soil until the structure is standing securely.

4. Plant climbing plants around the perimeter of the obelisk. You may have to secure non-clinging vines to the obelisk with ties. You can also attach garden netting to the obelisk to get a very full tepee effect.

Down to Earth
STATUARY MUSHROOMS

They attend conventions in the round on manicured lawns and slumber in the rich loam of oak tree roots until awakened by the prodding of well-trained snouts. They can be stuffed, sliced, sautéed, or even slyly recruited as murderous accomplices. Who'd have thought that the gilled fungi we call mushrooms could have such a colourful résumé?

While not all varieties of mushroom are welcome in the yard (or on the palate), these concrete replicas lend a whimsical statement to any landscape. The moulds are easy to source—all that's required is an assortment of bowls and some plastic baseball bats. In fact, these engaging mushrooms are so magically simple to make that the toughest part might be knowing when to stop production. Although these shy, concrete cousins lead slightly less romantic existences than their live counterparts, they are sure to make you smile all summer.

TIMELINE
1 week or less
(excluding curing time)

VALUE
DIY $100
Suggested retail $250

MATERIALS
14" and 26" hollow plastic baseball bats or bowling pins
Plastic bowls of various depths ranging from 6" to 12"
Two 24-gal. bags vermiculite or perlite
Four 55-lb. bags play sand
One 88-lb. bag type HS or 50 Portland cement
Duct tape and electrical tape
10M Rebar, 24' long
1/2" PVC pipe, 3' long
Silicone spray
Acid stain
Concrete sealant

Note: You'll have enough cement and sand to create about 12 mushrooms, depending on the size of moulds you use.

TOOLS
Tape measure
Sharp utility knife or electric kitchen knife
Cut-off saw with metal-cutting blade
    (or an angle grinder)
Electric drill and paddle attachment
Three large utility pails
Spoon or spatula
180-grit sandpaper or a fine file
8 1/2-cup measure
    (a plastic ice cream container works well)
Spray bottles
Scrub brush

Safety equipment required. See page 10.

STEP BY STEP

1. To begin creating the moulds for the mushroom stems, use a sharp utility knife or an electric kitchen knife to cut off the tops of each bat. Next, cut off the bottoms of each bat above the ribbed grips. The final length of the moulds should vary between 10" and 20".

2. Cut each bat in half lengthwise, creating two separate pieces.

3. Holding the two pieces together, hinge the mould together by duct taping along the outside seam of one side of the bat. Open the mould (as you would a hotdog bun), and spray the interior with silicone, taking care not to spray the exterior. Close the mould and duct tape along the other side.

4. Seal the narrow neck of the bat with duct tape and cut a small slit in the centre of the seal to accommodate the rebar needed in the next step. Reinforce the entire mould with a wrapping of electrical tape.

5. For each mushroom stem, cut a piece of rebar using a cut-off saw or an angle grinder. Make each stem 6" longer than the mould (the extra length will be used to secure the mushroom cap at the top and to make a spike at the bottom). Insert rebar into the mould, pushing it 1–1$\frac{1}{2}$" through the slit in the sealed end. When the rebar is in position, use a piece of electrical tape to mark where it aligns with the top of the mould. This guideline will help you correct any shifting of the rebar when you pour the cement.

6. Fill a utility bucket with sand and securely bury the neck of the mould in the sand. This bucket will hold the mould in place while it's being filled. Set aside.

7. To create the moulds for the mushroom caps, measure the depths of your bowls and for each, cut a piece of PVC pipe that is $1/2$" shorter than the bowl's depth. Place duct tape over one end of each of the pipe pieces and set aside. Spray the bowl interiors with silicone.

> **CAUTION:** Concrete is caustic, so follow the manufacturer's directions for safety. Refer to page 13 for information on working with concrete. Because concrete can be difficult to mix, make it in small batches. This recipe yields enough concrete to make approximately three mushrooms.

8. In a large pail, mix dry ingredients for the concrete. Using the $8^{1}/_{2}$-cup measure, scoop in three parts sand, three parts vermiculite, and three and a half parts cement. Mix well. Using the $8^{1}/_{2}$-cup measure again, fill another large pail with two parts water. Add the dry ingredients to the water, in small amounts. After each addition, blend thoroughly with the drill-mounted paddle. Continue adding dry ingredients until concrete resembles coarse oatmeal.

9. Spoon concrete into stem moulds and gently churn the rebar so that the concrete falls into place, topping it up, if necessary. (Varying the amount of concrete per stem will create an assortment of finished heights.) Adjust the vertical position of the rebar (using the tape mark as a guide), then position the rebar in the centre of the mould and secure it in place with duct tape.

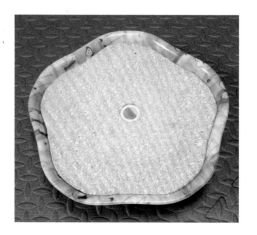

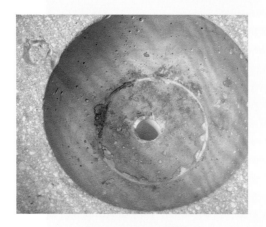

ALTERNATIVE METHOD: You can create a thinner, lighter mushroom cap by nesting a small mould inside of a larger mould. First spray the inside of the large mould and the exterior of a small mould with silicone. Then half fill the large mould with concrete and press the PVC pipe (taped on both ends this time) into the concrete, leaving $1/2$" of concrete between the end of the pipe and the bottom of the mould. Fill the small mould with sand and nestle it into the larger mould. Be sure to maintain a minimum space of 2" between the two moulds and not to allow concrete to cover the top of the pipe.

10. Fill cap moulds with concrete. With taped end facing down, press a piece of PVC pipe into the centre of each mould, being careful to leave $1/2$" of concrete between the taped end of the pipe and the bowl. Ensure the pipe is level with the concrete, but do not allow any concrete to get into PVC pipe.

11. Let concrete cure for 18–24 hours. Remove all the electrical tape and duct tape, open bats and remove stems. Invert bowl moulds and tap gently until caps release. Smooth out seams and rough edges with sandpaper or a file.

12. Assemble the mushrooms and place in a shaded outdoor spot. Leave them there for one week, wetting them down daily with a garden hose to allow the concrete to cure slowly. This treatment will increase strength and reduce shrinkage. Allow 24 hours drying time after final wetting.

13. Apply acid stain according to manufacturer's instructions. Dry 24 hours. Use water and mild detergent to rinse and scrub off acid residue. Repeat stain-and-wash process until desired effect is achieved. After a final rinse, dry for 24 hours. Finally, apply two coats of concrete sealant to prevent fading.

14. Arrange mushrooms in your garden or on your lawn, using the rebar spikes to secure them in place. Sit back and let these fungi grow on you!

A Work of Heart
HANGING CONE BASKET

Every gardener is an artist. Trading berets and brushes for straw hats and trowels, these designers work on a canvas so vast that a wheelbarrow is often required. With bare hands they boldly plunge green thumbs into untamed territory to create masterpieces with palettes of planting material. These originals often take months to complete, but the diligent never stray from their vision—combatting calluses and insect bites without missing a stroke. Compositions in this evolving gallery continually transform under the artistic guidance of their creator, sunshine, and washes of aqua. But a gardener's work is never done. A new canvas will beckon, and another scented art exhibition will materialize through the handiwork of these horticultural hobbyists.

This cone-shaped basket is an imaginative alternative to a traditional moss-lined container. Sculpted from stucco mesh, moss, and twigs, it can be suspended from brackets or attached to walls to give your outdoor space a gallery feel. This is a simple project that should take two to three hours to complete, giving you plenty of time to make more than one on an industrious Saturday afternoon.

TIMELINE
2–3 hours

VALUE
DIY $10
Suggested retail $55

MATERIALS
2 x 2' stucco mesh
Sheet moss
Soilless potting mix
Slow-release fertilizer
12 thin twigs, $^1/_4$–$^1/_2$" in diameter, 24" long
20-gauge wire
Six black tie wraps *(or 20-gauge wire)*
Three wire clothes hangers
Paper *(for pattern)*
Carabiner or S-hook
Water-retaining crystals *(optional)*
Raffia or twine *(optional)*

TOOLS
Wire cutters
Needle-nose pliers
Hammer
Heavy work gloves
Felt pen

STEP BY STEP

1. Create a pattern on paper to fit stucco mesh, or enlarge and use the template supplied below. Transfer the pattern to the stucco mesh using a felt pen. Wearing gloves, cut mesh with wire cutters.

2. Fold over sharp edges of mesh with needle-nose pliers and hammer flat. To form the cone, join the straight sides by slightly overlapping the mesh and whipstitching the seam closed with wire.

3. Bend twigs around the rim of the planter and fix in place with tie wraps or wire. Cover tie wraps with raffia or twine if desired.

TIP
Create pliable twigs by soaking them in a tub of water for several hours. This treatment will make them easier to bend around the rim.

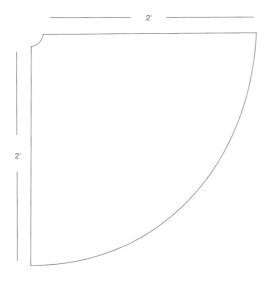

WHAT'S INSIDE

The shape and material of this basket are what make it interesting, so don't fill it with plants that will cover these features. In the image above, I've used *Osteospermum* 'Symphony Orange', which has a nice upright form, and *Petunia* 'Madness Midnight', which is much more compact than the trailing varieties of petunia that have become so popular. I've used two of each plant and found that my basket filled out quite nicely in just a few weeks. In the image on the opposite page, I used *Calibrachoa* 'Alpha Orange', a spider plant, and two asparagus ferns.

TIP

If packaged sheet moss has faded or turned brown, soak it on a cookie sheet filled with a strong solution of green food colouring for one hour. Drain excess liquid and dry on a rack for several hours.

4. Dampen sheet moss slightly (a spray bottle works well) and begin lining the cone, starting at the bottom. Be sure the moss is at least 1" thick on all sides.

5. Prepare the soilless potting mix by mixing in 1 cup slow-release fertilizer and, if desired, 2–3 tbsp of water-retaining crystals. Begin filling the moss-lined portion of the cone with potting mix. Continue adding moss, layer by layer, while filling with more potting mix, stopping 1" from the twig rim.

TIP

Use several wine corks in the foot of each cone to lighten the container (by decreasing the amount of soilless potting mix required) and to improve drainage.

ENJOY LIFE OUTSIDE

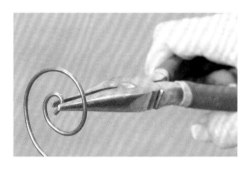

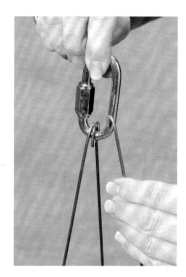

6. Using wire cutters, remove the necks and hooks from the clothes hangers. Straighten the hangers. With needle-nose pliers, bend one end of each wire into a decorative spiral loop.

7. Thread the straight end of the hangers through the rim of the cone under the twig edging. Once through, bend the top portion of each hanger to form a hook and attach to a carabiner or an S-hook.

8. If you prefer to hang your basket on a wall, omit the hangers and secure an S-hook at the back of the planter. (Remember to reposition the S-hook and turn the basket occasionally to promote even growth of plants.)

9. Add your favourite plants and water thoroughly.

Stand Your Ground
PRIVACY SCREEN

The benefits of stretching, meditation, and breathing have brought stress in your life to an all-time low. You have become addicted to this non-toxic high, melding mind, body, and soul in an ancient ritual with the odd chant thrown in for good measure. The only barrier between you and eternal bliss is the neighbour's kitchen window, which enjoys a clear view of your outdoor yoga mat. However, yoga is not about self-absorption. It's about love, compassion, and the right actions, and your new-found spiritually—with the help of an attractive screen— will enable you to attain privacy without borders.

This "good neighbour" screen can make your yard a true sanctuary, perfect for divine exercises or a little alone time. A collection of bamboo stakes or willow branches framed by perforated lumber can be hinged for mobility or permanently installed as a harmonious partition. Leave it unfinished or stain it to complement other surfaces. This versatile structure can also be installed indoors to create a division between rooms or as a backdrop for an intimate seating arrangement.

TIMELINE
4–6 hours

VALUE
DIY $100
Suggested retail $200

MATERIALS
Six 2 x 4" cedar or pressure-treated boards, 8' long
2¹/₂" deck screws
Exterior wood glue
Four 2¹/₂" pin hinges
100 bamboo garden stakes or willow branches, 6' long
Exterior stain or deck sealant *(optional)*
Upholstery tacks *(optional)*

TOOLS
Circular, chop, or table saw
Sander
150-grit sandpaper
Electric drill
2" hole-saw bit
¹/₁₆" drill bit
Paintbrush
Tape measure
Straight edge

Safety equipment required. See page 10.

STEP BY STEP

1. To create the three frames that make up the screen, begin by cutting six 48" pieces of lumber for the sides. Then cut nine 32" pieces for the tops and bottoms.

2. Sand all pieces and wipe clean.

3. Lay six of the 32" pieces on their wide side. Mark a centreline across the entire length of each piece. Next, mark 2^1/$_2$" in from either end of each piece on the centre line. Divide the area left between these marks into eight equal measurements, 3" apart, to end up with 10 cross marks on each board. These marks will serve as the centre of each bored hole.

4. Drill each hole with the hole-saw bit halfway through the board. Flip over and repeat. Sand and wipe the edges of the holes. Save and set aside the cut-out pieces.

TIP

When using a hole-saw bit, begin boring into the wood on a slow speed until the teeth have made even contact with the wood surface. Increase the drill speed and push with moderate pressure until you have reached top speed. Slow the drill speed occasionally and pull the hole-saw bit out of bored hole to clear any sawdust that has accumulated inside. This will prevent the drill from jamming. Drill half way through the board and then flip the board over and align the hole-saw bit with the pilot hole on the underside. Continue drilling until the hole-saw bit has cleared the board.

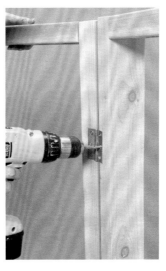

5. Create the frame bottoms by joining a board with holes to a solid board. (Doubling the bottom rung prevents the stakes from falling through and provides extra weight for stability.) Start by lining up a board with holes parallel to a solid board. Position a straight edge evenly between each hole and mark the solid board. These marks indicate where to screw the two boards together. Next, apply glue to the saw-drilled unit and place the solid board on top, marked side up. Drill pilot holes for screws with $^1/_{16}$" bit and affix with wood screws.

6. Place side pieces on the outside ends of the frame bottom and top so the finished panel will measure 48" high. Pre-drill two pilot holes at the top of each side piece and four at the bottom. Glue and screw the side pieces in place. Cover screw heads with upholstery tacks if desired.

7. Space the cut-out pieces from the bored holes evenly along both sides of the bottom of the frames. Affix with deck screws. Stain or seal the frames if desired.

8. The completed panels are hinged together at their sides. First, mark the hinge placement 8" from the top and bottom of each panel. Pre-drill pilot holes and install the hinges to create a folding screen.

9. Drop bamboo stakes or willow branches into the holes of the top panels and fit into the ends into the bottom panels.

10. Position the screen to provide privacy and level to provide stability.

Go with the Flow
GARDEN SHOWER

The air is dry and tastes of heat. You glance at the treetops for any sign of movement, but everything is still. The mercury has tipped the 35°C mark and forecasts indicate no relief from the heat wave despite rumbling empty promises of nightly thundershowers. Heat shimmers into a bleached sky and then plunges back to earth with blistering vengeance, day after scorching day. The familiar sounds of summer are absent—most of the neighbourhood has disappeared into air-conditioned digs or cool basements. You briefly entertain the thought of biking to the pool but break into a sweat just pondering it. A cold shower seems like a more favourable solution.

If you don't have the luxury of a pool to cool off in, consider a portable outdoor shower instead. This playful device is a great way to combat soaring temperatures (or rinse off muddy feet) right in your own backyard. Although this is a challenging project, I've eliminated the need to use an intimidating acetylene torch by substituting with solderless bonding adhesive. There's no need to stain the cedar mat or protect the copper pipe because they will age to soft silver and a verdigris patina, respectively, in a few short seasons. Drain and store this portable unit indoors over winter.

TIMELINE
8 hours
(excluding curing time)

VALUE
DIY $125
Suggested retail $200

MATERIALS
Large plastic planter
18 cups type 50 Portland cement
36 cups play sand
Decorative rock
Ten 1 x 2" cedar boards, 8' long
1¼" deck screws
½" type M rigid copper pipe, 3' long
Two ¾" type M rigid copper pipe, 3' long
¾ x ¾" piggyback valve
    (brass hose attachment)
¾" stop valve
    (brass tap to control water flow)
Two ½" copper pipe end caps
¾" copper pipe end cap
Three ½" to ¾" copper pipe adapters
½" showerhead adapter
¾" stainless steel shower flange
6" diameter rain showerhead
1" PVC pipe, approximately planter height
5' x 12" C-110 (.010") copper sheet
Just-for-Copper solderless bonding adhesive
Plumber's Teflon tape

Double-sided tape
Masking tape
Duct tape
Garden hose with two female ends

TOOLS
Pipe cutter
Hacksaw
Funnel
½" pipe bender *(available at rental outlets)*
Rasp or file
Electric drill and paddle attachment
¹⁄₁₆", ½", 1", and 1¼" drill bits
Two utility pails
Measuring cup
Spatula
Rubber mallet
Level
Scissors
Needle-nose pliers
Cut-off or chop saw
Heavy work gloves

Safety equipment required. See page 10.

ENJOY LIFE OUTSIDE

STEP BY STEP

1. Begin by creating the shower gooseneck. Cut two 2" pieces of $^1/_2$" copper pipe with the pipe cutter or hacksaw. Remove any burrs with rasp or file. Set aside for shower assembly. Place one $^1/_2$" end cap on remaining 32" piece of pipe. Fill the pipe with sand using a funnel. Cap the remaining end and duct tape both caps onto the pipe securely. Wrap the pipe with three layers of duct tape. This treatment will prevent any scratching or marring from the pipe bender.

TIP

You can replace the copper pipe with a shower riser designed for use with claw-foot tubs. The pipe is usually 5' long with a 10" gooseneck projection.

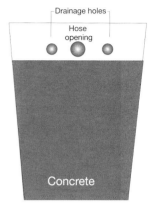

Drainage holes

Hose opening

Concrete

2. Place one end of the pipe in the pipe bender and begin flexing pipe according to supplier's directions. Take your time with this step. Copper pipe tends to kink very easily; bending slowly and evenly will prevent this problem. Once you have achieved the desired curvature, remove duct tape and end caps, and empty the sand out of the pipe, reserving it for the concrete mixture.

3. Next, create the shower base. Drill a hole with the $1^{1}/_{4}$" drill bit 2" below the top of the planter. This is where the garden hose will be inserted. Then, drill two holes with the $^{1}/_{2}$" drill bit on either side of the hose opening for drainage.

Caution: Concrete is caustic, so follow the manufacturer's directions for safety. Refer to page 13 for information on working with concrete.

4. Measure and cut the PVC pipe to 2" below the hole for the garden hose. Cover one end of the PVC pipe with double-sided tape and centre it on the interior bottom of the planter.

5. Concrete placed at the bottom of the planter provides stability. In a large pail, mix the cement and sand. Fill another large pail with 10 cups of water. Add the dry ingredients to the water, in small amounts. After each addition, blend thoroughly with the drill-mounted paddle attachment. Blend until the mixture resembles coarse oatmeal. Pour into the planter, stopping 1" from the top of the PVC pipe. Tap sides of planter with a rubber mallet to tamp concrete into nooks and to self-level the top of the pour. Insert a long piece of copper pipe in the PVC pipe. Place the level alongside the PVC pipe and adjust as needed. Allow concrete to cure for 24 hours. Remove the copper pipe.

Enlarge to 12"W x 21"H

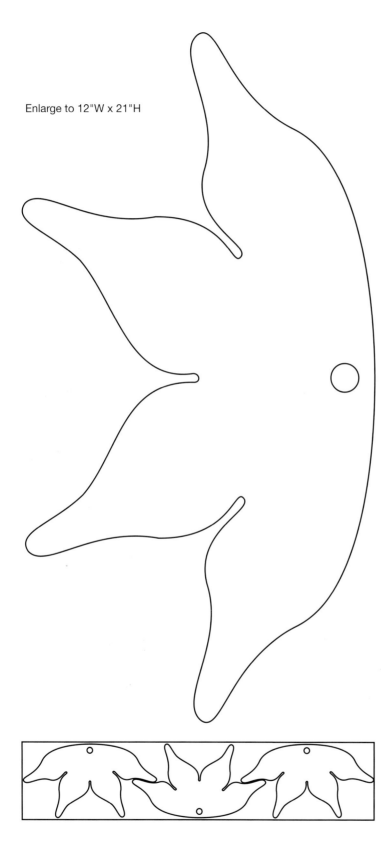

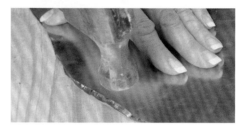

6. To create the shower head, begin by enlarging the pattern *(left)* to 12" x 21". Transfer three copies of the pattern onto the copper sheet according to the template layout below. Wearing gloves, cut out shapes with scissors.

7. Drill a hole with the 1" drill bit in each cut-out as outlined on the pattern. File off any burrs or rough edges. Fold a ¼" hem around each leaf set with needle-nose pliers and hammer flat.

TIP
Copper sheets are available at metal superstores, which are located in most major cities. These outlets purchase leftover materials from metal fabricators and resell to the public in small quantities.

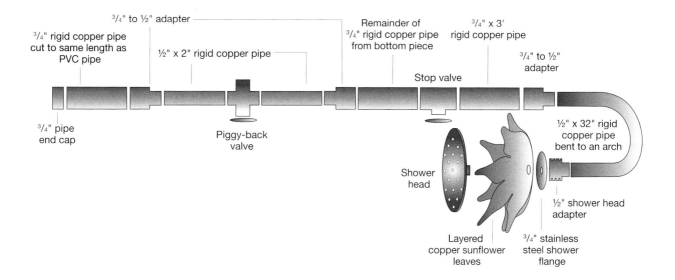

3/4" to 1/2" adapter

3/4" rigid copper pipe
cut to same length as
PVC pipe

1/2" x 2" rigid copper pipe

Remainder of
3/4" rigid copper pipe
from bottom piece

3/4" x 3'
rigid copper pipe

3/4" to 1/2"
adapter

Stop valve

3/4" pipe
end cap

Piggy-back
valve

1/2" x 32" rigid
copper pipe
bent to an arch

Shower
head

1/2" shower head
adapter

Layered
copper sunflower
leaves

3/4" stainless
steel shower
flange

8. To create the shower assembly, cut the 3/4" copper pipe to the same length as the PVC pipe. Lay out the shower components as illustrated. Prepare and bond all joints, with the exception of the showerhead, with Just-for-Copper according to the manufacturer's directions.

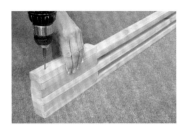

9. Shape sunflower leaves over the shower head by bending gently. If the leaves appear to spin freely on the shower head collar, pinch the opening edges together to tighten the leaves against the collar. Place flange over leaves. Apply Teflon tape to the shower head threads and screw onto the shower head adapter.

10. To create the cedar mat, cut 16 pieces 40" long and 30 pieces 8" long from the cedar boards.

11. With the $^1/_{16}$" drill bit, pre-drill pilot holes 1" from each end of the 8" pieces and $1^1/_2$" from each end of the 40" pieces. Assemble the mat by sandwiching two short pieces between long pieces. Using $1^1/_4$" deck screws, attach an 8" piece to each end of a 40" piece. With the 8" piece in place, attach another 40" piece to this unit. Continue as outlined in the drawing at left.

Cedar mat

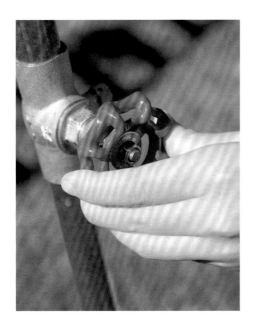

12. Place cedar mat in desired location and position planter at one end. If you are placing the mat on uneven ground, put boards under each end to create a solid base. Drop the shower assembly into the PVC sleeve. If the assembly is loose in the PVC pipe, wrap the bottom of the unit in duct tape until a snug fit is achieved. Feed the garden hose through the opening of the planter and attach to the piggyback valve of shower assembly.

13. Disguise the concrete by filling the top of planter with decorative rock.

14. Turn on the water supply at the building and open the piggyback valve on the garden shower. Adjust water flow to shower head with the stop valve.

No Stone Unturned

PEBBLE RELIEF PAVERS

Vacations have you stuck between a rock and a hard place. Roadside landslides, babbling brooks, and abandoned abodes have become the "stone superstores" for your hardscape material needs. With a keen eye for organic art, you have created a "hard rock" buffet of winding dry creeks, retaining walls, and a bedrock populace of Inuksuit that stand guard over a carpet of woolly thyme. These found objects are not just a collection of building blocks—they are mementoes of moments in time, souvenirs of places, people, and pinnacles you have parlayed into paradise. Rock on!

Use your precious finds to fabricate these decorative pavers, which can be displayed individually or grouped for a stunning patio centrepiece. I've included enough materials to create four pavers and one convenient mould that can be re-used for multiple pours. If you're keen to make more than one paver at a time, create as many moulds as you desire, but continue to only mix one batch of concrete at a time for ease of process. One more word of advice: go easy on your back when lifting and placing pavers. Use a wheelbarrow or cart for hauling. Oh, and don't forget, picking rocks from national parks is against federal law. If your pebble inventory is running low, check out dollar stores or landscaping suppliers for washed river rock or polished stone.

TIMELINE
2–3 hours
(excluding curing time)

VALUE
DIY $15 per paver
Suggested retail $80

MATERIALS
20 x 20" melamine-coated $5/8$" particleboard
$1^1/_2$" wood screws
Silicone caulk
35 lbs. type 50 Portland cement
35 lbs. play sand
River rock or pebbles
Two 12 x 12" pieces of thin plywood, cardboard or Fome Cor

TIP
Melamine-coated particleboard has a resin finish that releases very easily from cured concrete, making it ideal for paver moulds, but you can replace melamine with plywood if you seal the wood with several coats of sealant or glossy paint and use a generous amount of release agent (spray silicone) with each pour.

TOOLS
Table, chop, or skill saw
Two large utility pails
Electric drill and paddle attachment
$1/_{16}$" drill bit
Caulking gun
Plastic measure
Spatula
Hammer or rubber mallet
Level

Safety equipment required. See page 10.

NOTE
You'll have enough cement and sand to create four pavers.

STEP BY STEP

1. To create the mould, cut one 12 x 12" bottom from the melamine particleboard. Then cut two $2^1/_2$ x 12" pieces and two $2^1/_2$ x $13^1/_4$" pieces for the sides.

2. Pre-drill all screw pilot holes and attach side pieces to bottom unit with screws as illustrated. Lay a bead of silicone on all seams to seal the mould. Cure at least four hours.

3. Draw your design on one of the two 12 x 12" boards and lay out the stone pattern.

4. Prepare the concrete recipe for one tile as follows. In a large utility pail, mix 9 cups of cement and 9 cups of sand. In a second pail, pour $3^1/_2$ cups of water. Add the dry ingredients to the water, in small amounts. After each addition, blend thoroughly with the drill-mounted paddle. Continue adding dry ingredients. The concrete will resemble coarse oatmeal.

5. Place the mould on a level surface. Pour concrete into mould and spread it evenly with the spatula. Using a hammer or mallet, gently tap the sides of the mould until the concrete has settled into the corners.

CAUTION: Concrete is caustic, so follow the manufacturer's directions for safety. Refer to page 13 for information on working with concrete.

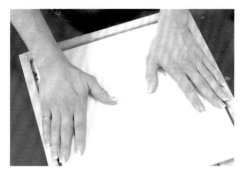

6. Place rocks into cement in desired pattern. If your pattern involves straight lines, use straight edges as guides for the design. Larger rocks will have to be embedded deeper in the mix.

7. Place the second 12 x 12" board in mould and firmly press stones until level.

8. Cover filled mould with plastic wrap and allow concrete to cure for 24 hours.

9. Unscrew and remove one or two sides of the mould and ease the paver out with a spatula. Scrub the surface of the paver with a stiff brush and water to remove any concrete accumulated on rocks. Cure concrete seven days before setting pavers in ground.

10. Re-attach the sides of the mould and seal seams with silicone before pouring additional pavers.

11. To prepare the ground for the pavers, dig down approximately 3–4" and level the surface. Pour a base of sand approximately 1–2" deep and level the surface. Place each paver on top of the sand, nestle it into place, and level as required.

Pots and Whatnots
PRACTICAL POTTING BENCH

It's January. Blowing snow pummels frosted windows as gale-force winds tear through the city. You spend exactly 20 seconds contemplating shovelling the walks before a shrieking kettle requires your attention. A pot of tea and a stack of magazines you have been hoarding will provide an afternoon of indulgent escapism. Nothing solaces a gardener's soul during the dead of winter as much as poring over seed catalogues, planning the spring garden. Like a pocket of collected seeds waiting for the ideal conditions to germinate, you spring back to life, preparing and plotting a landscape strategy. This is your day...drifts on the sidewalk can wait.

Whether you are sowing seeds or repotting plants, a potting bench is ideal for any garden devotee. Craft this multi-purpose workstation from recycled ingredients—a bathroom cabinet, louvered shutters, and a bi-fold door. Source materials at your local Habitat for Humanity ReStore and reduce materials headed for landfills, support building programs for those in need, and construct a practical fixture in the process. My version is fairly elaborate (the benefit of taking this project up a notch means that it can double as an attractive outdoor buffet), but you can simplify as desired, perhaps using a recycled laminate countertop or a varnished door instead of the tiled countertop. Mine is placed on the patio under a roof where it is largely protected from the worst weather.

TIMELINE
10–20 hours
(excluding drying time)

VALUE
DIY $100
Suggested retail $350

Safety equipment required. See page 10.

MATERIALS
Bath or kitchen base cabinets
Four 5" wheels, two with brakes
Louvered shutters or louvered bi-fold doors
Bi-fold door panel *(solid)*
2 x 4" lumber, 8' long
Four shelf brackets
2 x 2' fine hardware wire mesh
2 x 4' piece $^3/_8$" plywood
1", 2", and 2$^1/_2$" deck screws
16 washers *(size to correspond with heads of the screws selected)*
Staples
S-hooks
Plastic trash can or storage bin

OPTIONAL MATERIALS
Trisodium phosphate (TSP)
1 qt. exterior paint or stain
Latex glaze
Burnt-umber tint
Deck sealant
RedGard waterproof membrane
Tile

Mastic tile adhesive
Grout
Grout sealant

TOOLS
Skill or table saw
Jigsaw
Electric drill
$^1/_{16}$" and $^3/_8$" drill bits
Pencil
Stapler
Hammer
Wire cutters
Heavy work gloves

OPTIONAL TOOLS
Sander
150- and 180-grit sandpaper
Paintbrush
Tile cutter
Spatula
Notched trowel
Grout float
Sponge
Pot scrubber

TIP
Gently used dressers, bureaus, or desks can be substituted for cabinetry. If the unit has a top drawer, select an appropriately sized plastic food storage container or, alternatively, forgo the container and simply coat the interior of the drawer with deck sealant.

STEP BY STEP

1. If the cabinet unit has a sink, remove it (the void left will be covered with a removable mesh cover for potting). To create a hole in a solid top, trace an oval-shaped opening onto the counter. Drill a pilot hole with the $^3/_8$" drill bit to provide a starting point for the jigsaw blade. Cut out with the jigsaw.

2. Flip the cabinet over and determine wheel placement. Cut wheel supports to length from the 2 x 4" lumber. Attach the supports to cabinet with 2" screws, and then attach wheels to supports with washers and screws. Pre-drill all screw pilot holes.

3. If the cabinet, shutters, or bi-fold doors require refinishing, remove all hardware and sand with 180-grit sandpaper, then stain or paint with at least two coats of selected finish. If an aged patina is desired, mix burnt-umber tint with latex glaze and dry-brush onto painted surfaces. Seal all finished surfaces with deck sealant. Replace the hardware.

4. If you have opted to tile over a laminate countertop instead of leaving it as is, it is preferable to remove the laminate, but it is not absolutely necessary—as long as you prepare the laminate surface properly. Try removing the laminate with a hammer and spatula. If the adhesion is too strong, move on to prepping the laminate for tiling. First, wash the counter with a trisodium phosphate (TSP) solution using a pot scrubber; rinse well. Next, sand with 150-grit sandpaper and wipe with a damp cloth to remove any dust. If you are applying tile directly onto wood, seal all surfaces with two coats of RedGard waterproof membrane. Dry-fit your tile design on the countertop and cut tile to fit. Apply mastic with a notched trowel to the surface according to manufacturer's instructions. Set tile in place. Allow tile to set for 24 hours.

Mix grout according to manufacturer's directions and apply grout between tiles. Allow grout to dry for 24 hours, clean surface and seal. Repeat process with solid bi-fold door panel if you've opted to tile its upper surface. For more information on tiling, see page 15.

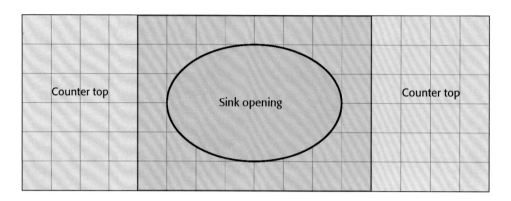

Counter top

Sink opening

Counter top

Removeable cover and
under-counter support (Trace 2)

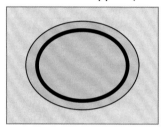

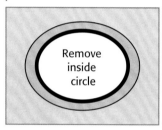

Remove
inside
circle

Removeable cover

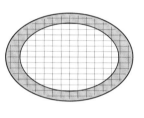

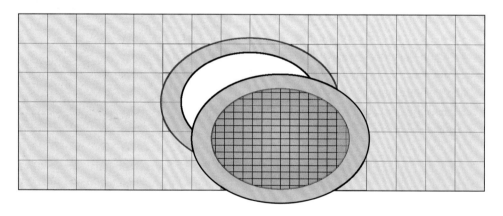

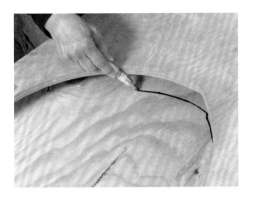

5. To create the frames of the removable sink cover and its under-counter support, first trace two outlines of the sink opening on the plywood sheet. Within each outline draw a second outline $1^1/_2$" from the first line. Cut the frames out by drilling a pilot hole with the $^3/_8$" drill bit to provide a starting point for the jigsaw blade. Cut out along the inner line first, then along the outer line. Paint or stain the pieces. Centre one frame to the underside of the sink opening and attach with 1" screws. Wearing gloves, cut hardware wire mesh to fit the other frame with wire cutters, staple onto the removable cover, and hammer staples flat against mesh. Place cover, staple side down, over sink opening and placc plastic storage bin under opening in cabinet.

6. To create the potting bench's backboard, trim the shutters or louvered bi-fold doors to required height. Attach each panel to the cabinet's back using $2^1/_2$" screws spaced 6" apart to ensure a stable base for mounting shelves.

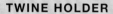

TWINE HOLDER

Keep twine accessible with this handy holder. Cut 6" from the centre of a wire clothes hanger with wire cutters. Slip a spool of twine onto one exposed end and crimp just below the neck of the hanger to bring the cut ends together within the spool.

7. Screw shelf brackets at desired height onto the frames of the shutters or louvered bi-fold doors with 1" screws. Place the solid bi-fold door panel on the brackets to create a shelf.

8. Attach S-hooks to louvers to hang garden implements and place seed packages or photos between slats.

A Drop in the Basket
FREESTANDING HARVEST CATCHALL

The popular pastime of hosting social gatherings in yards, on driveways, or in garages has become synonymous with diverting household items from landfills while offering bargain seekers adrenalin rushes. This weekend ritual usually involves residents spreading wares on rickety tables and frayed blankets in the hopes of scoring a profit while lightening their homes of the unused and unwanted. Advertising for these exclusive retail opportunities usually comes in the form of handwritten signs posted around the neighbourhood. Although this practice may seem primitive to some, garage sale aficionados across the land gleefully empty their piggybanks as they barter for treasures.

Garage sales sport chaotic jumbles of items crudely sorted into categories—a perfect opportunity to gather scrap lumber, a woven basket, and a broomstick or cane to create this handy skewered basket. It is the ideal accompaniment in the garden while gathering fresh cutflowers, veggies, or fragrant herbs. This simple project will enhance the joy of reaping what you've sown.

TIMELINE
1 hour

VALUE
DIY $10–20
Suggested retail $50

MATERIALS
Woven basket with a handle

$1\frac{1}{8}$" dowel, broom handle, or cane, 4' long

$\frac{1}{8}$" hardboard or Masonite, twice as large as basket base

$\frac{5}{16}$" dowel, as long as the diameter of the basket bottom plus 2"

150-grit sandpaper

Small fence post finial

TOOLS
Pencil

Jigsaw

Sander, sanding block, or knife

Finishing wax or exterior stain

Electric drill

$\frac{1}{8}$", $\frac{5}{16}$", and $1\frac{1}{8}$" drill bits

Hammer

Safety equipment required. See page 10.

ENJOY LIFE OUTSIDE

STEP BY STEP

1. Make a pattern of the basket bottom and transfer two copies to the hardboard or Masonite. Cut out with a jigsaw. Drill a $1^{1}/_{8}$" hole in the centre of the basket bottom and both wood pieces.

2. Hone, sand, or whittle one end of the $1^{1}/_{8}$" dowel, broom handle, or cane to a point and sand smooth. Stain or wax the stake and the fence post finial to protect and let dry.

TIP
Periodically clean soil from the stake and seal with finishing wax or stain to prevent the wood from deteriorating.

3. Push the stake through one wood piece, then through the basket bottom, and finally through the second wood piece until the stake's flat end reaches the basket handle. Mark the stake where it meets the interior of the basket bottom and again on the exterior of the basket bottom to determine where holes will be drilled for the plugs that will hold the stake in place and provide support. Remove the stake and drill holes for the plugs with $5/16$" drill bit. Drill a pilot screw hole with $1/8$" drill bit into the flat end of the stake for the finial.

4. Cut the first plug dowel to the width of the exterior wood base and set aside. Hammer the remaining length of dowel into the top hole of the stake, closest to the flat end. Assemble by sliding a wood piece onto the pointed end of the stake up to the plug, followed by the basket, and then the second wood piece. Hammer the remaining plug into the stake beneath the basket to support the basket bottom.

5. Push the mounting screw for the fence post finial through the basket handle and screw it into the pre-drilled hole at the top end of the stake.

HARVESTING

There's no greater joy than harvesting what you've grown.

I prefer to cut flowers for arrangements in the early morning or evening. I find that the stems are firmer and the flowers seem to hold up better than they do when gathered in the heat of the day.

Vegetables are at their finest when they're picked just prior to preparing. I prep all of my other menu items first, then whip out to the garden to cut lettuce, pluck beans, or snip herbs. Fresh!

Pillow Talk
SNAPSHOT CUSHIONS

Icelandic poppies fight for legroom in my overcrowded garden, occasionally relocating with self-sown abandon to the more spacious quarters around the gazebo. Asiatic lilies peek out from the lacy veil of lady's mantle, their gentle grace almost lost in the profusion of colour and texture. What a shame that the stage for these performers is seasonal. There's no business like sow business. Fortunately, I am lucky enough to enjoy this riot of flora year round through a little digital ingenuity.

Turn your favourite snapshots into comfortable works of art to dress up an otherwise plain sofa or chair. This project requires the most basic of photography and sewing skills, but yields custom pieces to be treasured for years to come. Colour-coordinate your fabric choices to work with both your indoor and outdoor décor and get even more value for your designing dollar. Here's how I harnessed the glories of my garden.

TIMELINE
3–5 hours

VALUE
DIY $65–75 per cushion

Suggested retail $125 per cushion

MATERIALS
Digital photos
Cushion forms
Fabric for front of cushions *(supplied by commercial printer)*
Fabric for back of cushions *(a durable cotton or polyester, pre-washed to prevent shrinking)*
Thread
Self-adhesive Velcro coins
Piping or cording *(optional)*

TOOLS
Digital camera
Sewing machine
Zipper foot *(optional)*
Scissors
Tape measure
Iron

STEP BY STEP

1. Purchase cushion forms that are of the appropriate size for your project.

2. With your camera set at high resolution, photograph a panoramic view of your garden, and save it to a disc at 300 dpi. If your image will not span over several cushions, take a number of photos of one vista, moving the camera slightly in one direction with each frame.

3. To determine the size of fabric needed for each cushion front, measure your cushion form and add ³/₄" on each side for seam allowances. Source a local printer and order the images to the appropriate dimensions. For a photo pillow with a matte finish, request polyester fabric; for a polished look, order taffeta.

4. Cut fronts of cushion covers from the printed fabric, using the measurements determined in Step 3. If desired, use a zipper-foot to attach piping to the right side of each front panel (raw edges of fabric and piping together). Set cushion fronts aside.

5. To create backs for the cushions, cut panels from the unprinted fabric, using the measurements from the fronts but adding 8" to the top edges. For example, if fronts are 15 x 15", backs will be 15 x 23". Cut back panels in half, width-wise, and on either side of the centre cuts, fold edges over 2" (wrong sides together). Iron flat.

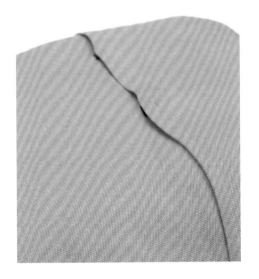

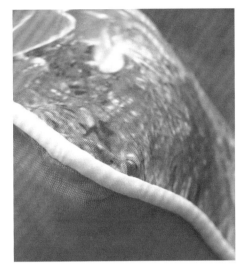

6. With right sides facing up, overlap the split back panels to create squares that are the same size as the fronts. Pin backs to fronts (right sides together), and stitch ³/₄" from edges all around the perimeter.

7. Turn right sides out, and add Velcro coins to the back overlap sections to prevent gaping.

8. Stuff cushion covers with cushion forms, arrange on sofa, and sink into the comfort of your garden.

Sittin' on the Fence
CUSTOM CANVAS GARDEN

They toy with your imagination, this travelling gallery of natural abstract expressionists. Constantly re-inventing themselves, the eclectic group is known simply as Cumulus, Stratus, and Nimbus. They roll across an infinite blue canvas that inspires you to rediscover the artist within. A towering wedding cake, a well-groomed poodle, and a skateboarder morph before you in a series titled "White on Blue." Blink, and the installation transforms to a new exhibit. Gallery hours fluctuate on wind-powered technology. Once the gusts move in, the aerial show dissipates, and it's time to get your head out of the clouds.

Create a permanent exhibit for your outdoor living space with bold canvases generated from cherished photos of your garden—or someone else's. The reasons to tackle this easy project are many. If your outdoor living space is limited to a paved side yard or a tiny balcony, this may be the best instant (and maintenance-free) garden ever. If you can't afford a significant piece of statuary, who's to say you can't own a two-dimensional copy? And finally, if you're leaving a treasured garden behind in a move to downsize and simplify, this project allows you to create a lasting, but manageably sized, memento. Go on. Dress up bare walls or jazz up bland fences, and put yourself on cloud nine.

TIMELINE
2–3 hours

VALUE
DIY $50–75

Suggested retail
$125–200

MATERIALS
Digital photo

2 x 2" cedar or pressure-treated lumber
(amount determined by desired frame size)

2¹/₂" deck screws
(Or purchase canvas stretchers from an art supply store and forgo the above materials)

⁵/₁₆" staples

Exterior wood glue

Packing or duct tape

Picture hanging kit (optional)

TOOLS
Chop or hand saw

Electric drill

¹/₈" drill bit (Or purchase canvas stretchers from an art supply store and forgo the above tools)

Digital camera

Square

Stapler

Tape measure

Hammer

Scissors

Safety equipment required. See page 10.

STEP BY STEP

1. Take a high-resolution digital photo of a scene you want to recreate on canvas and save it to a disc at 300 dpi for images up to 24 x 24" and 600 dpi for larger photos. Source a local sign printer and order images printed on banner material to desired measurements. Specify UV-tolerant outdoor inks for outdoor art so that the image will stand up to the elements without fading for at least five years. You can also request a laminated protective finish on your canvases for extra durability.

2. If building your own frame, measure the height and width of the canvas. Create the top and bottom frame pieces by cutting two boards 5" smaller than the height of the canvas. Create the sides for the frame by cutting two boards 8" less than the width of the canvas.

   Pre-drill a pilot hole on each end of the top and bottom pieces. Set the side pieces on the bottom piece and align the top piece, making sure the frame is square. Glue and screw the frame pieces together. Measure and cut out four mitred corner braces for each frame. Pre-drill pilot holes, and glue and screw the braces in place.

If using canvas stretchers for the frame, purchase them large enough to allow you to wrap the canvas around the frame without exposing the edges of the canvas to view when the project is hung. Glue and assemble the stretchers and ensure that the frame is square. Position a staple gun so that the staples will straddle the joints where the stretchers meet. Staple twice at each corner and let the glue dry before proceeding.

3. Lay the canvas face-side down on a blanket or carpet, and centre the completed frame on top. Always start stapling at the centre point of each side. Begin attaching canvas to frame on one side. Wrap the canvas around the frame edge to the backside of the frame and staple about 1" in from the edge of the canvas. Staple right up to the corners. Stretch material and repeat on the opposite side.

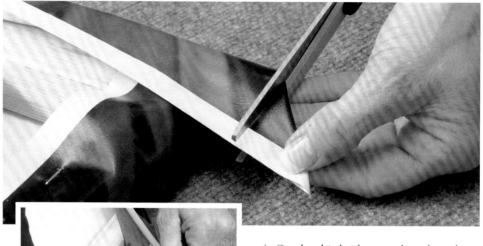

4. On the third side, stretch and staple material onto the frame as directed in step 3, but stop 2" short of the corners. Repeat with the last side. Flip canvas over and check for wrinkles and adjust stretching as necessary.

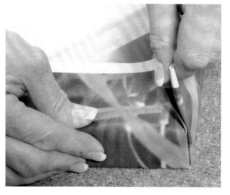

5. Pulling the canvas taut at the corners as illustrated, cut off the excess canvas to prevent bulk. Tautly pull one edge and fold over the frame. Hold this edge in place while pulling and folding the remaining edge over. Staple onto frame. Once again, flip over and check for wrinkles or creases. Adjust if required.

6. Hammer all staples into the frame so that they are flush with the wood, and cover them with packing or duct tape to prevent scratching surfaces when hanging the canvas and to waterproof the staples, which otherwise may rust and stain surfaces.

7. If required, trim excess canvas edges.

8. Hang the completed project directly by the frame or by attaching hangers to the frame. Mount on a fence or wall and toast your artistic success.

Ripple Effect
STACKED TRICKLE FOUNTAIN

The alarm went off at six this morning and you've been on the go ever since. You've put out fires at work, fought freeway traffic for hours, and prepared a hearty meal for the troops. You linger over the pile of mail on the counter long enough to realize that there is nothing but bills. Sigh...time to retune your mind, body, and soul. Pour yourself a tall cool one, head outside, and plop into your favourite chair where the bustle of the city slowly dissipates behind a gentle trickle of water. The day's stress and strain pours out of you with every drop. You take a sip of your drink and survey the horizon. Suddenly, life seems...well, pretty darn good—at least until tomorrow morning's alarm.

Personalize your outdoor sanctuary with a creative water feature fashioned with the help of everyday plastic food savers. The slender stacked fountain rises from a compact trough—perfect for small spaces. I've including enough materials for a four-foot high fountain, but the height and the colour of the finish are ultimately determined by your preference. The silicone caulk used to hold the layers together can be removed to take the unit apart, allowing you the freedom to relocate or store the water feature with ease.

TIMELINE
2 weeks *(excluding curing time)*

VALUE
DIY $175–225
Suggested retail $350–450

MATERIALS
Scrap lumber *(if moulds are flimsy)*

Containers for moulds
🅐 9 x 9" plastic food savers 2", 3", and 4" deep for stacking blocks
🅑 5 x 5 x 5" square container, for overflow block, to fit into an 🅐 mould
🅒 for pump block *(larger than profile of fountain pump)*, to fit into an 🅐 mould

Two containers for base trough
🅓 15 x 22 x 10", to fit into container 🅔
🅔 18 x 24 x 10"

Two 88-lb. bags white Portland cement
Reinforcement fibres
Five 55-lb. bags play sand
1" PVC pipe, 4' long
¹/₂" PVC pipe, 4' long
Silicone spray
Masking tape
Double-sided tape
Acid stain
Concrete sealant
Silicone caulk
Fountain pump, no more than 170 gallons (U.S.) per hour
Flexible hose to match pump requirements, 4¹/₂' long

TOOLS
Hacksaw
Two utility pails
Electric drill and paddle attachment
Spatula
Measuring cup
File
Kitchen blowtorch
Spray bottles
Scrub brush
Caulking gun
Level

Safety equipment required. See page 10.

TIP
You can use type 50 Portland grey cement, which is considerably less expensive than white cement. It produces a darker finish when stained and sealed.

Overflow block

Stacking blocks

Pump block

Base trough

STEP BY STEP

This fountain consists of four main parts: a base trough at the bottom of the fountain to circulate water; the pump block, which acts as a shelter for the pump; a collection of stacking blocks that provide the fountain's elevation (pour as many as you require for desired finished height); and an overflow block at the top of the fountain from which the water trickles.

1. Build simple wood frames or cradles from scrap lumber for any containers that may bulge when filled with concrete. Place the containers in the frames. If the moulds are made of sturdy plastic, you can omit this step.

2. Begin by creating the stacking blocks for the middle of the fountain. Place a straight edge on top of each mould Ⓐ determine the length of the 1" PVC pipe, which the fountain's flexible tubing will pass through. Cut the appropriate lengths from the 1" PVC pipe. Seal one end of pipe with masking tape. Using double-sided tape, seal the other end and adhere this end to the bottom of the mould. Position the pipe slightly off centre to create the fountain's staggered effect. Spray the interiors of the moulds with silicone.

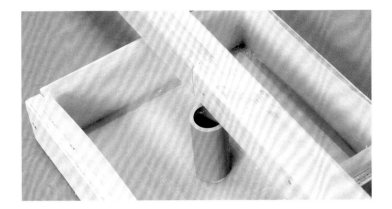

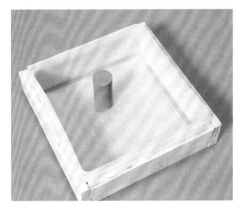

TIP
A concrete colourant can be added to the recipe to achieve a uniform colour instead of acid staining which produces a leathery, mottled look.

3. In a large pail, mix the cement and sand. In another large pail, pour the water. Add the dry ingredients to the water, in small amounts. After each addition, blend thoroughly with the drill-mounted paddle attachment. Continue blending until concrete resembles coarse oatmeal. If mix becomes too dry or difficult to work with, add a bit more water.

4. Keeping the PVC pipe standing straight, scoop the concrete mix into mould with the spatula, and massage lightly into corners. Do not over-work; leaving some voids in the concrete will give an aged patina to the finish. Drag a piece of lumber across the top of the filled mould to even out the concrete. Make sure the PVC pipe stays level. Allow the concrete to set for 24 hours. Invert the mould, remove the block, and file any rough edges.

CAUTION: Concrete is caustic, so follow the manufacturer's directions for safety. Refer to page 13 for information on working with concrete. Because concrete can be difficult to mix, it helps to make it in small batches. The first recipe below yields enough concrete to make approximately one 9 x 9 x 2" concrete block **Ⓐ**. If you want to make more than one block at a time, follow the second recipe as a guide and eyeball the yield for the number of blocks you want to make. Either way, the mixing method remains the same.

6 cups sand	*or*	3 parts sand
12 cups cement		6 parts cement
4 cups water		2 parts water

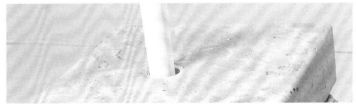

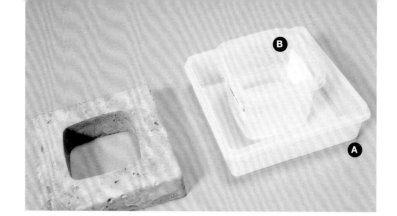

5. Create the mould for the overflow block by using two containers—a smaller container centred inside of a larger container. Centre container **B** inside of **A** and secure to the bottom of **A** with double-sided tape. If necessary, secure at edges where containers meet with additional masking tape. Spray the void between the containers with silicone. Using the same recipe as used for one stacking block, mix and pour concrete as previously directed. Allow to set for 24 hours. Remove the inner container **B**, invert, and remove the block from the **A** mould. File any rough edges.

6. The pump block, which sits in the base trough and conceals the fountain pump, must be big enough to house the pump assembly. To create this u-shaped block use two appropriately sized containers—a smaller container **C** placed inside a larger container **A** and secured to one side with double-sided tape. If necessary, secure at edges where containers meet with additional masking tape. Spray the void between the containers with silicone. Using the same recipe as used for one stacking block, mix and pour concrete as previously directed. Allow to set for 24 hours. Remove the inner container **C**, invert, and remove the block from the **A** mould. File any rough edges.

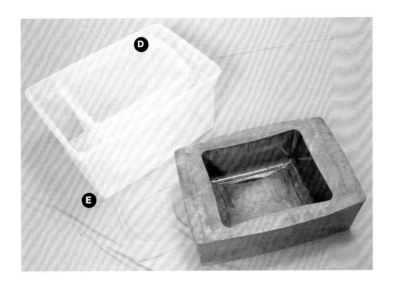

7. The base trough holds the water that is circulated up through the fountain and it must be large enough to hold the pump block. To create this mould, use two appropriately sized containers—a small container **D** positioned in a larger container **E** to make a sink-like impression.

The recipe below will produce half the amount of concrete required for the trough. Smaller batches are more manageable to work with, but be sure to mix and pour the second batch immediately following the first batch to ensure binding with first pour. Mix the concrete as previously directed but add the reinforcement fibres to the other dry ingredients. Add a small amount of water if mix becomes too dry.

21 cups sand

42 cups cement

5¼ cups reinforcement fibres

17½ cups water

Spray the inside of the large container **E** with silicone. Pour approximately 2" of concrete into the mould. Tamp the mould. Spray the exterior of container **D** with silicone and centre it inside of container **E**. Weigh it down with enough sand or concrete to hold it in place but not to sink it to the bottom of the container **E**. Mix the second batch of concrete. Pour the concrete mix in the void between the two containers and tamp lightly to level. Level the inner container and trowel the surface of concrete with the spatula to smooth. To reduce the porosity of the trough, continue to smooth every hour until concrete has hardened (approximately four hours). Allow to set for 24 hours. Remove the inner container **D**; then invert and remove outer container **E**. File any rough edges and use a kitchen blowtorch to burn off any fibres that sit proud of the concrete surface.

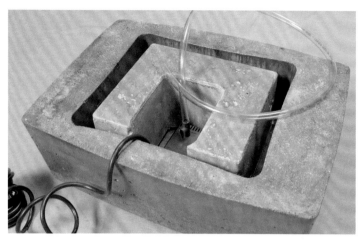

8. After all units have cured for at least one week, apply acid stain with spray bottles according to manufacturer's instructions. Mix several colours together to create a natural, mottled look. Dry 24 hours. Rinse and scrub off acid residue in a water bath with mild detergent. Repeat stain-and-wash process until desired effect is achieved; the more stain you apply, the darker the finish. After the final rinse, dry 24 hours and apply two coats of sealant to prevent fading. Apply an additional coat of sealant inside the base trough.

9. Select a level location for the fountain. Place pump block in base trough and insert the pump. Next, position one of the stacking blocks over the pump block and insert the 4' length of ½" PVC pipe into the opening. This rigid pipe will provide additional stability to the fountain and create a channel for the flexible pump hose. Continue positioning the stacking blocks. Mark the finished height on the PVC pipe if it extends more than 1" from the top stacking block. Once you are pleased with the overall profile, number the blocks, and dismantle the fountain. If necessary, cut the PVC pipe with the hacksaw. Reassemble the fountain, adding a small bead of silicone caulk between each layer. Be sure to level each layer (use additional silicone if necessary). Crown the fountain with the overflow block. Caulk the space between the PVC pipe and the top stacking block.

10. Feed the flexible pump hose down the PVC pipe and attach the bottom end to the pump. Fill the base trough with water and turn on pump. Adjust flow as desired.

WATER PLANTS
Although the base trough of this fountain isn't very large, there is room for a few water plants to finish the piece off. Some small plants worth trying are water lettuce (*Pistia stratiotes*), water hyacinth (*Eichornia crassipes*), and the really tiny—despite its name—giant duckweed (*Lemna* spp.).

Gaining Ground
PERFECT PEDESTALS

Despite your diligent efforts and carefully calculated beds, plants gleefully escape their confines regularly. Some days you don't have the energy to fight the wave of impudent chaos and simply shrug your tired shoulders and walk away. A young brood of smug delphiniums wink at each other in victory. Maltese cross giggle at their triumph. A cluster of false sunflowers huddles together, planning a strategy to break new ground in the shale path. Perhaps the time has come to take charge and re-establish order. And then you spot it: an unlikely yet happy marriage of rampant rhubarb and bleeding heart setting up house in a forgotten corner of the yard. A poised arch of dangling valentines is a striking complement to the ruffled foliage and maroon stems. You wonder why you hadn't thought of pairing them yourself. So many possibilities, so little space.

Gain a little ground in your garden with pedestals that will allow you to display statuary or plants artfully in decorative pots. The open design of these contemporary pedestals introduces an architectural element to any landscape without weighty obtrusion. I've included enough material to make three pedestals. Grouping them in sets of odd numbers produces a more pleasing composition. If you like, make an extra set to use as end tables for the patio or deck. If you are feeling particularly creative, tile the tops with a favourite mosaic and make each pedestal a work of art in its own right. Copy my finish choice or choose a colour that works for you.

TIMELINE
8–10 hours
(excluding drying time)

VALUE
DIY $95
Suggested retail $200

MATERIALS
Eleven 2 x 4" pressure-treated or
    cedar boards, 8' long
Three 4 x 8' sheets $^3/_8$" pressure-treated or
    exterior-grade plywood
Exterior wood glue
$1^1/_2$" finishing nails
$2^1/_2$" deck screws
Exterior wood filler *(plastic wood)*
150- and 220-grit sandpaper
Exterior stain-killer bond paint
1 qt. copper-toned exterior latex paint
    (base coat)
Copper metallic spray paint
4 oz. light teal exterior latex paint
    (verdigris patina)
1 qt. deck sealant

> **NOTE:** You will have enough material for three pedestals.

TOOLS
Table saw or circular saw
Electric drill
$^1/_{16}$" and $^3/_8$" drill bits
Hammer
Jigsaw
Nail punch
Sander
Spatula
4" paint roller
Sponge or rags

Safety equipment required. See page 10.

TIP
Always wear eye protection and a respirator when cutting or sanding pressure-treated wood to avoid irritation from preservatives.

STEP BY STEP

1. Cut the 2 x 4" lumber as follows for two pedestals **Ⓐ**:
   Eight pieces 7$\frac{1}{4}$"
   Eight pieces 19$\frac{1}{4}$"
   Sixteen pieces 29$\frac{3}{4}$"

   Cut the 2 x 4" lumber as follows for pedestal **Ⓑ**:
   Four pieces 14$\frac{1}{4}$"
   Eight pieces 22$\frac{3}{4}$"
   Four pieces 26$\frac{1}{4}$"

2. For two pedestals **Ⓐ**, cut and label the plywood as follows:
   Four pieces 12 x 6$\frac{1}{4}$" (inside)
   Four pieces 12 x 19$\frac{3}{8}$" (top, bottom)
   Four pieces 12 x 20$\frac{3}{4}$" (inside)
   Four pieces 12 x 33$\frac{3}{4}$" (sides)
   Four pieces 20$\frac{3}{8}$ x 33$\frac{3}{4}$" (front, back)

   For pedestal **Ⓑ**, cut and label the plywood as follows:
   Two pieces 12 x 13$\frac{1}{4}$" (inside panels)
   Two pieces 12 x 13$\frac{1}{2}$" (inside panels)
   Two pieces 12 x 25$\frac{3}{4}$" (top, bottom)
   Two pieces 12 x 27$\frac{1}{4}$" (sides)
   Two pieces 26$\frac{3}{4}$ x 27$\frac{1}{4}$" (front, back)

3. Build four frames **Ⓐ** and two frames **Ⓑ**. Using the illustration as a guide, assemble each starting with the H-shaped centre and then adding the exterior sides. Where pieces join or intersect, pre-drill two pilot holes with the $\frac{1}{16}$" drill bit, then drive in the deck screws and countersink.

Ⓐ

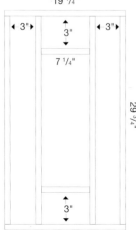

19$\frac{1}{4}$"

◄ 3" ► 3" ◄ 3" ►

7$\frac{1}{4}$"

29$\frac{3}{4}$"

3"

Ⓑ

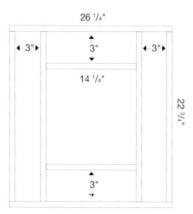

26$\frac{1}{4}$"

◄ 3" ► 3" ◄ 3" ►

14$\frac{1}{4}$"

22$\frac{3}{4}$"

3"

4. Place two frames together and align with the outside edges of the corresponding top and bottom plywood pieces. Glue and nail the plywood pieces in place. Next, affix the plywood sides as above. To secure the long inside panels, glue in place and then hammer the nails in at an angle. Flip the entire unit over and hammer the nails in at an angle on the other side. Glue and nail the short inside plywood pieces in place.

5. Lay the pedestal on top of the front plywood piece and mark off the centre opening of the pedestal. Drill a pilot hole with the $^3/_8$" drill bit to provide a starting point for the jigsaw blade. Cut out with the jigsaw and repeat process with back plywood piece.

 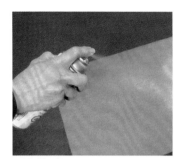 

6. Attach front and back plywood to pedestal with glue and nails as directed above. Countersink all nail heads with nail punch. Repeat this assembly process for the other pedestals.

7. Sand pedestals with 180-grit sandpaper. Fill nail holes, crevices and knots with wood filler. Dry four hours. Sand with 220-grit sandpaper. Top off any remaining blemishes with filler, if required, and sand once more. Wipe clean.

8. Seal pedestals with two coats exterior stain-killer bond paint and dry for 24 hours.

9. Apply two coats of basecoat with roller and dry for eight hours. Spray metallic copper paint randomly on all surfaces and dry for two hours. Mix verdigris paint half and half with water and apply to surfaces with a rag. Use a circular motion to rub paint into base coat, then smooth out by wiping paint with the wood grain. Mottle any strokes with a dry sponge until finish is smooth and seamless. Dry 24 hours.

10. Protect finish with two coats of sealant and dry for 24 hours.

11. Place pedestals on a level surface in the garden, arranging them horizontally or vertically, as you like.

The Lighter Side
PATIO LANTERNS

The stars are out tonight. Not the Hollywood kind that sashay the red carpet in a quest for Oscar, but the variety that announce night's arrival in a show of twinkling lights. You settle in for an evening of stargazing in your personal amphitheatre as the dark velvet of night descends. The constellations are cued up. A quick game of connect-the-dots delineates the Dippers as you search for the North Star. A shooting star streaks by, and you quickly make a wish before it disappears—maybe this time it will come true. The repertoire of a distant owl announces the arrival of a tuxedoed moon that has joined the star-studded cast. Unquestionably, the performance merits an Academy Award.

Create a series of perpetual twinkling stars from strings of outdoor mini-lights and vellum paper. These lights can edge a hedge, decorate an arbour, or encircle a terrace after the sun has retired for the evening. Not only is this an easy project to execute but also one that can change with the theme of any outdoor event you may host, or decorating scheme you may hatch.

TIMELINE
1–2 hours

VALUE
DIY $25

Suggested retail
$45

MATERIALS
Five to seven sheets 12 x12" vellum paper

50-count string exterior mini-lights or exterior LED lights

Electrical tape complementary or matching colour to vellum

5 yds. fine-gauge wire or 50 small tie wraps

TOOLS
Pencil

Scissors

Ruler

Needle-nose pliers

Wire cutters

*Light shade template
shown actual size*

TIP
By all means, display light strings without overhead protection, but be prepared to take them down to prevent damage from rain.

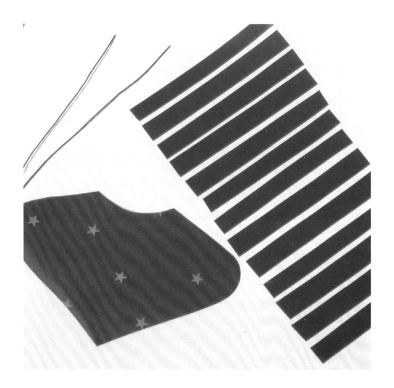

STEP BY STEP

1. Transfer template of light shade pattern (on page 110) onto vellum and cut out 50 copies.

2. Cut electrical tape into 3" strips, and then cut each strip in half lengthwise. Lay the strips on a surface such as laminate that allows you to peel them off easily as you work.

3. Attach tape to inside radius of shades, leaving a $^1/_2$" of tape free on each side, as illustrated. Gently stretch tape to follow the curve.

4. Adhere each shade to a mini-light socket, creating a cone around each light.

5. Using needle-nose pliers, reinforce the taped base with 4" of wire or a small tie wrap. Hang the lights, plugging in to an exterior-rated extension cord if required.

Wine, Dine, & Thine
CHILLING AND TASTING TABLES

Entertaining in the garden is a seasonal joy not to be missed. The hours you may spend in the kitchen are always rewarded at the patio table as the wine flows alongside good conversation and full-bodied laughter. The rhythm is relaxed as course after course makes its appearance to rave reviews. Bizet's Carmen *fills the air as secrets are shared and bonds are re-established. Kudos! Another successful dinner party is under your culinary belt—well worth the army of pots and pans that surely waits in the kitchen.*

I present here—for your entertaining pleasure—two versions of a handy table that can be used for chilling and serving beverages. Designed to provide ample storage space for glasses, decanters, and corkscrews, either is the perfect companion for your next garden party. One version incorporates a battered old bedside table covered in mementoes of fine bottles long gone. The other is composed of a combination of newly constructed and repurposed parts. Use your creativity to dream up alternatives of your own—perhaps using paper coasters, wine labels, or deconstructed wine crates?

Cork-itecture

WINE CORK TABLE

This table is a perfect example of a project that you really can simplify and personalize. I've covered the entire table in corks, but you might choose only to cover the top and instead paint the rest. You may also choose to skip the plastic food saver/would-be-ice-holder and place ice directly into the cooler—an option that means that you can use a table base without a drawer.

Although this version is sealed to help protect it from the environment, it's best stored with a roof overhead. It is light enough to cart out to the lawn for an event and move back at the end of an evening. A corky theme makes it the perfect conversation piece outdoors, in your dining room, or, if you're lucky enough to have one, wine cellar.

TIMELINE
8–10 hours
(excluding drying time)

VALUE
DIY $10–50

Suggested retail
$125–150

MATERIALS
End table with drawer *(drawer optional)*
180-grit sandpaper
Tapered galvanized flower bucket or wine cooler *(top wider than bottom)*
Corks
Wooden-handled corkscrew
Two 1½" wood screws
Hot glue sticks
Spray polyurethane
Plastic food saver to fit drawer *(optional)*

TOOLS
Sander or sanding block
Rag
Measuring tape
Pencil
Bandsaw
Jigsaw
Electric drill
⅛" and ¼" drill bits
Utility knife
Glue gun

Safety equipment required. See page 10.

TIP
To cut several corks efficiently, I created a jig from a scrap piece of 2 x 4" lumber with a small channel grooved into the centre to hold the corks. I clamped a guide onto the band saw and placed the jig beside it. I then lined up the wine corks on the jig and safely fed one after the other into the band saw to cut in half.

STEP BY STEP

1. Begin by sanding the glossy surfaces on the end table. Wipe clean.

2. Determine where you want the flower bucket or wine cooler to rest in the table. Measure the circumference of the container at this spot. Trace a corresponding circle onto the centre of the tabletop.

3. Drill a pilot hole in the circle with the $1/4$" drill bit to provide a starting point for the jigsaw blade. Cut out the circle with the jigsaw and sand any rough edges.

4. Cut corks in half, taking care to preserve the winery markings. Hot glue the cork halves onto the table, including to the inside lip of the cut-out. Cut any mitred corners or custom length pieces with the utility knife.

5. Apply two coats of polyurethane to corked surface. Dry for 12 hours.

6. Pre-drill holes on the handle of the corkscrew with $\frac{1}{8}$" drill bit and attach to drawer with screws. Cut two thin circles from a cork and glue over the screws to conceal.

7. To use, fill the plastic food saver with crushed ice, place it in the drawer and insert the bucket into the tabletop. Add a bottle of choice and let the party begin.

WINE LABEL HOLDER
Use any leftover halved corks as place card holders for the dinner table or as label holders at your next wine and cheese. Simply cut an angled slit with a utility knife and insert a card.

Table Wine

TILED TASTING TABLE

This table was created by constructing a sturdy box from plywood to support the tile, but there are many other options for both construction and finishing. Consider substituting a wine or produce crate as the tabletop. Wine shops, flea markets, and your local grocer are great sources. Preserve the crate's history by applying several coats of deck sealant on the interior and exterior of the crates. If the crate is on the plain side, you can decoupage wine lists or labels, or even photos of significant "toasts" to the surface. Attach wheels to your table's legs and make the unit mobile for movable feasts.

TIMELINE
6–8 hours
(excluding drying time)

VALUE
DIY $100–175
Suggested retail
$150–175

MATERIALS
Two 24 x 48" pieces $1/4$" plywood
Two 2 x 2" boards, 8' long
Exterior wood glue
Two galvanized flower buckets or wine
 coolers
Four antique legs or spindles
$1^1/_2$" and $2^1/_2$" deck screws
Four large washers *(size to correspond
 with heads of the screws selected)*
Stain
Finishing wax
Mastic tile adhesive
7–8 sq ft of 1 x 1" and 2 x 2" mosaic tiles
Unsanded grout
Grout sealant

TOOLS
Table saw or circular saw
Electric drill
$1/_8$" and $1/_2$" drill bits
Tape measure
Pencil
Jigsaw
Sander or sanding block
180-grit sandpaper
Paintbrush
Tile cutter or wet saw
Tile nippers
Spatula
Grout float
Notched trowel
Sponge
Rags

Safety equipment required. See page 10.

TIP

Tiling is an easy way to customize pieces of outdoor furniture. The sheer variety of kinds, colours, and, yes, even shape of tile readily available is vast. Here, I've gone for contrast between a deep chocolatey-brown mosaic tile and a lighter tumbled faux stone tile, but alternatively you could paint the base and top it with clear glass mosaic tiles for a modern feel. Or you could salvage a favourite chipped china plate and flattened cutlery to create a mock place setting. Have fun with it.

STEP BY STEP

1. From the plywood, cut the following and lightly sand any rough edges:

   Two pieces 16 x 24" *(top and bottom)*
   Two pieces 7½" x 24" *(long sides)*
   Two pieces 7½" x 16" *(short sides)*

2. From the 2 x 2" lumber, cut the following:

   Ⓐ Four pieces 24" long

   Ⓑ Four pieces 12" long

   Ⓒ Four pieces 4" long

   Ⓓ Four pieces 2 x 2" long *(leg supports)*

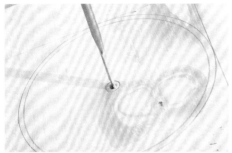

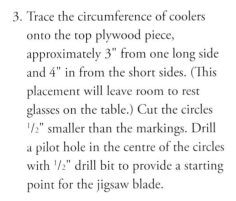

3. Trace the circumference of coolers onto the top plywood piece, approximately 3" from one long side and 4" in from the short sides. (This placement will leave room to rest glasses on the table.) Cut the circles $1/2$" smaller than the markings. Drill a pilot hole in the centre of the circles with $1/2$" drill bit to provide a starting point for the jigsaw blade.

4. Lay out the top and bottom plywood pieces. Glue the **A** pieces to the long sides of the plywood and the **B** pieces to the short sides. Flip the units over and pre-drill screw holes with the $1/8$" drill bit, approximately every 6", and secure pieces with $1^1/2$" screws.

5. Lay out the two long plywood side pieces. Centre and glue the **C** pieces to the edges of the short sides of the plywood. Flip the units over and pre-drill two evenly spaced screw holes with the $1/8$" drill bit and secure pieces with $1^1/2$" screws.

6. Attach the long side units to the bottom unit. Pre-drill screw holes with the ⅛" drill bit and secure with 1½" screws. Repeat to attach the short plywood sides to the bottom unit.

7. Stain the interior and exterior of the bottom unit by brushing on stain and ragging off excess. When dry, apply wax, and buff.

8. Sand and stain the cut-out edges of the tabletop unit, the legs, and the leg supports. Wax the legs for added protection. Set aside.

9. Pre-drill a pilot hole through the centre of each leg support and into the top end of each leg with the ⅛" drill bit. Glue the leg supports to the inside corners of the bottom unit. Centre a washer over the leg support's pilot hole and then drive a 2½" screw through the support, the bottom unit, and into a leg that has been pre-glued.

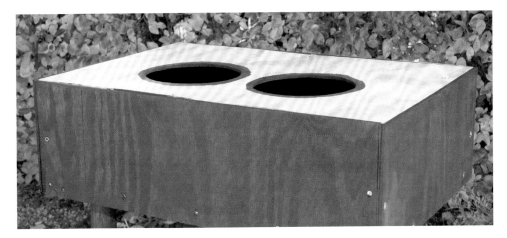

10. Attach the top unit to the bottom unit. Pre-drill pilot holes with the $^1/_8$" drill bit, and glue and screw into place.

11. Dry-fit your tile design onto the tabletop. Begin at the top's edges and allow tile to hang over edge enough to cover the exposed edges of the tile you will place along the table's sides. Work in toward the cooler cut-outs. Cut tile to fit, using nippers to shape tiles around the openings. Apply mastic tile adhesive according to manufacturer's instructions. Start at the back of the unit and trowel mastic to plywood. Transfer the tiles onto the adhesive, gently pressing down. Allow tile to set for 24 hours. Mix grout according to manufacturer's directions and apply grout between tiles. Allow grout to dry for 24 hours, clean surface, and seal. (For more information on tiling, see page 15.)

12. Fill coolers with crushed ice, insert into the tabletop, and chill your favourite beverage.

Scrap Gold

VOTIVE, TEA LIGHT, AND VASE HOLDERS FROM LEFTOVERS

A chipmunk's survival strategy is relatively simple. Gather as many sunflower seeds as possible from under a bird feeder, then hide the harvest for a rainy day. With bulging cheeks, the striped crusaders race about the yard in search of the perfect location to bury their stash. Unfortunately, these dexterous collectors often forget about their stockpiles, leaving them to germinate in the most unlikely places. In no time, the fruits of their labours produce seedlings that pop up in window boxes, shale paths, or right in the middle of a manicured lawn.

Interestingly enough, we are guilty of the same behaviour. We hoard bits and pieces and often forget about them. Lumber scraps from various undertakings collect dust in the corner of the garage or workshop, but we don't have the heart to trash them. The time has come to transform that pile of scraps into perfect accessories for home or garden—a collection of vase caddies, tea light holders, or votive vessels. Get rid of the leftovers; then go reorganize the garage.

TIMELINE
2–6 hours
(excluding drying time)

VALUE
DIY $5–10
Suggested retail
$30–40

MATERIALS *(For all models)*
1 x 2" lumber
2 x 4" lumber
4 x 4" posts
4 x 6" posts
Branches and twigs
1¹⁄₂" finishing nails
India ink
Craft paint
Exterior stain
Satin spray varnish
Gesso
1³⁄₄ x 7" diameter glass vases
1¹⁄₄ x 4" shooter glasses
Glass pebbles
Tea light holders *(votives)*
Tea lights
Upholstery studs
Raffia
Tie wraps
Exterior wood filler
Exterior wood glue
Silicone caulk
Glue sticks
Finishing wax

TOOLS
Chop saw
Band saw
Electric drill or drill press
1¹⁄₂ and 2" Forstner bits
Mitre box
Sander or sanding block
80-, 150-, and 180-grit sandpaper
Hammer
Tape measure
Needle-nose pliers
Glue gun
Paintbrush
Rags
Wood clamps *(optional)*

Safety equipment required. See page 10.

Each of these projects should be kept out of the rain, waxed seasonally, and stored indoors over winter.

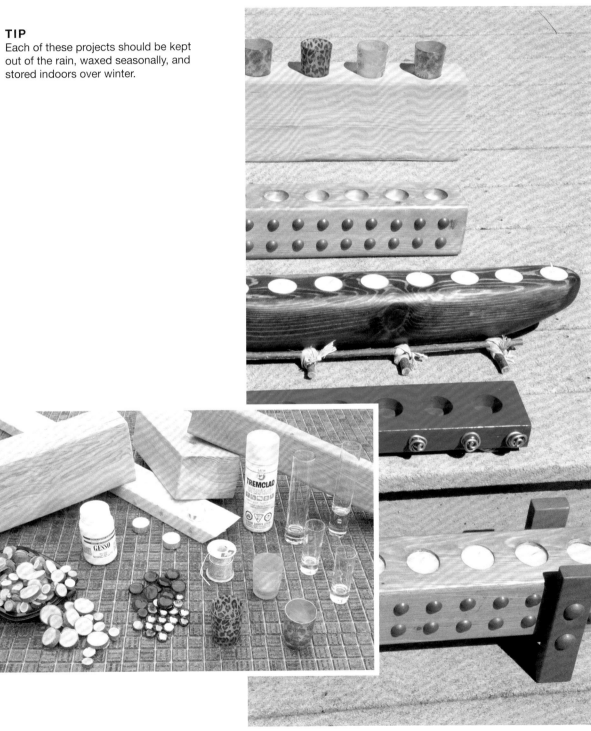

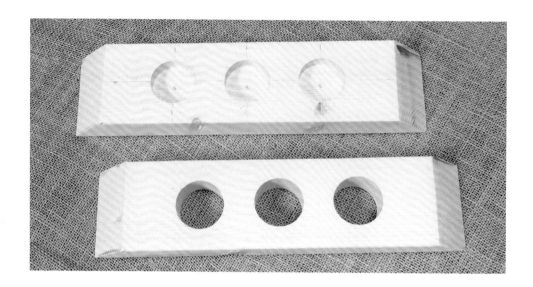

VASE CADDY

This caddy has the look of concrete due to its ultra-smooth surface and India ink finish. You can always substitute the vases for a collection of shot glasses that fit the openings.

STEP BY STEP

1. Using 2 x 4" lumber scraps, cut two 15" pieces for the top and bottom of the caddy, and two 5" pieces for the sides. To create a frame that fits together at the corners, mitre each end of each piece at a 45-degree angle as illustrated. Sand the pieces with 180-grit sandpaper and wipe.

2. Mark the midpoint of length and width to find the centre of each piece. On the top and bottom pieces only, mark two additional points 3" from either side of the center point.

3. Using the 2" Forstner bit, drill a hole at each marked point right through the top and side pieces. Place a scrap piece of wood under the pieces when drilling to prevent splintering on the underside. On the bottom piece, drill the holes only $1/2$" deep.

4. To create the frame, line up the corners and join the pieces with wood glue. Allow the glue to dry for 24 hours. Brace the sides of the caddy with sand-filled vases or use wood clamps until glue has set.

5. Fill any gaps on mitred corners with wood filler, allow to dry and sand smooth.

TIP

You can substitute a spade bit to drill the holes in these projects. However, while it costs considerably less than a Forstner bit, the spade will leave a cone-shaped hole at the bottom of each bore and could puncture thinner pieces of wood. The Forstner produces a clean, flat bottom and has less of a tendency to skip while drilling.

ENJOY LIFE OUTSIDE

6. Apply gesso with a paintbrush. Once dry, sand smooth. Repeat this process until caddy is completely smooth. Paint with white craft paint and dry overnight.

7. Mix equal parts of India ink and water to paint the entire caddy. Let dry 30 minutes. Add 10 percent more ink to the mix and add strokes of detail to create a mottled look. Let dry 30 minutes. Add another 10 percent ink to mix and paint the inside edges of the holes. You can continue adding ink detail until you have achieved a concrete or stone patina. If you've applied too much ink, wipe off the excess with a damp cloth. Let dry.

8. Set vases in the top holes and fill with fresh flowers from the garden.

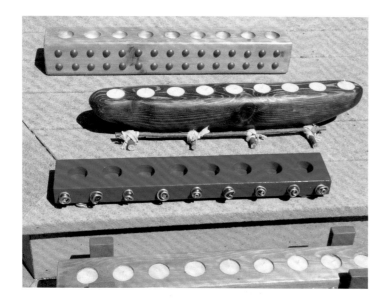

POST TEA LIGHT HOLDER

Alter the look of utilitarian square fence posts by laying them on their sides and supporting them with funky stands and cradles.

STEP BY STEP

1. Select a length of 4 x 4" scrap lumber. The length selected will determine how many tea lights the piece can accommodate. On one long side of the lumber, mark the midpoint of length and width to find the centre point for middle tea light. Then measure and mark off every $2^1/_2$" on the remainder of the board, which will allow a space of 1" between each tea light. Drill each hole $^5/_8$" deep with the $1^1/_2$" Forstner bit.

2. Leave the shape as is and simply sand the edges smooth, or use a band saw to hone the piece to a boat-like form. Start sanding with 80-grit sandpaper and finish with 180-grit.

3. Stain and wipe off excess. Dry 6 hours. Wax and buff.

4. Here are two options for displaying the holder: a twig cradle or a two-piece scrap-wood stand.

   To create the twig cradle, cut four twigs approximately 6" long and cut two twigs 4" longer than the tea light holder. Position the twigs as illustrated. Secure the twigs with tie wraps and cover with raffia.

   To create the two-piece stand, use 1 x 2" lumber scraps. Cut four 6" pieces for the stand's sides and two 5" pieces for the bottoms. Sand the edges and paint to a desired finish. Allow to dry. To assemble, position a horizontal bottom piece 1" from a side piece and nail in place. Attach the second side piece on the opposite end of the bottom piece. Repeat for the second stand. Embellish with upholstery studs.

5. Position the stands evenly under the votive holder. Insert tea lights directly into holes.

TIP
Make your own dark wax paste by adding a few drops of paint colour tint to a clear wax and mixing thoroughly with a spatula.

CHUNKY TEA LIGHT, VOTIVE, OR VASE VESSEL

Use pieces of 4 x 6" lumber vertically to create pedestals in a variety of heights for interesting centrepieces.

STEP BY STEP

1. Select a length of 4 x 6" lumber. Stand the lumber on one end. Mark the desired position of the holes for the tea lights, vases, or votives. Using the $1^1/_2$" Forstner bit, drill the holes $^5/_8$" deep for each tea light or 3" deep for each vase. For each votive holder, drill a $1^1/_2$" deep hole using the 2" Forstner bit.

2. Sand with 180-grit sandpaper and wipe. Leave the piece unstained for an interesting look.

3. Slice branches into coins of varying thickness with a band saw. Dry coins in a single layer on newspaper for 48 hours to ensure the wood will adhere properly. Attach to lumber with hot glue.

4. Insert tea lights, votives or vase holders.

TIP
Get creative with embellishments. You can use coiled 50/50 solder, pebbles, and even coins.

INDEX

ACKNOWLEDGEMENTS

This project would never have come to fruition without the vision and generosity of many people. I would like to thank the following:

My publishers, Bill and Valerie Hole, who believed in me from the beginning, for embracing my dream and giving me a chance to earn my first book credit;

My editor, Christina McDonald, whose foresight and perceptive editing kept the red ink flowing in a quest to keep it simple, and my photographer, Akemi Matsubuchi, whose creative eye captured the true essence of this volume through straightforward photography;

My husband, Harold Mueller, for his encouragement, positive spirit, and deep pockets;

My mother, Lilli, for getting dirty, breaking nails, and harbouring countless hot glue wounds in her quest to help me meet deadlines;

My colleague and friend, Barbara Deters, whose sage advice proved to be immeasurable and helped lay the groundwork, and for teaching me to write;

My brother-in-law, Gordon Mueller, who welcomed me into his workshop and offered savvy advice when obstacles and problems sometimes overwhelmed me;

And finally to my neighbours, Colleen and Lindsay McDougall, and Miss Julie Wheaton for allowing us to use their yards and for modelling.